GHOSTS of NEW YORK

GHOSTS
of NEW YORK

SUSAN BLACKHALL

THUNDER BAY
P·R·E·S·S

San Diego, California

Thunder Bay Press
An imprint of the Advantage Publishers Group
5880 Oberlin Drive, San Diego, CA 92121-4794
www.thunderbaybooks.com

Copyright © PRC Publishing 2005

An imprint of **Chrysalis** Books Group plc

All notations of errors or omissions should be addressed to Thunder Bay Press,
Editorial Department, at the above address. All other correspondence (author
inquiries, permissions) concerning the content of this book should be addressed to
PRC Publishing, The Chrysalis Building, Bramley Road, London W10 6SP,
United Kingdom.

ISBN 1-59223-414-3

Library of Congress Cataloging-in-Publication Data
available upon request.

Printed in Malaysia

1 2 3 4 5 09 08 07 06 05

Additional Captions
Page 1: Dancers of the Zeigfeld Follies. The theater where they performed
is now haunted by one of the Zeigfeld's most successful stars.
Page 3: Dylan Thomas enjoys a drink at the White Horse Tavern, his
favourite haunt.

contents

INTRODUCTION

"I took a large room, far up Broadway, in a huge, old building whose upper stories had been wholly unoccupied for years, until I came. The place had long been given up to dust and cobwebs, to solitude and silence. I seemed groping among the tombs and invading the privacy of the dead, that first night I climbed up to my quarters. For the first time in my life a superstitious dread came over me; and as I turned a dark angle of the stairway and an invisible cobweb swung its lazy woof in my face and clung there, I shuddered as one who had encountered a phantom."

"A Ghost Story"—Mark Twain

New York City, a teeming metropolis known the world over for the gritty sense of humor and no-nonsense approach of its natives. With its glass-fronted skyscrapers, constant bustle, and hard-nosed business acumen, it is the most unlikely city on earth to harbor ghouls and wraiths and spirits, and yet there are vast numbers of ghost sightings here. It seems that one is as likely to feel the icy breath of the dead or hear their whispering voices in this most modern of cities as in any tumbledown Transylvanian castle.

Of course, untold millions of people of all races and religions have lived and died in New York since the days when it was home to the Algonquin Native Americans. So it is perhaps inevitable that, in such a vast sea of people, there will be some who suffer tragedy or injustice grave enough to chain their spirits to the scene of their pain. There appear to be many reasons for a haunting—a few of which we will explore here—but the majority of ghosts are just such people. Rather than embrace the peace and rest of death, they linger, just touching our world enough to make their presence felt, hoping for some resolution to their pain. There is Lucy Ryan, for example, who starved to death, raped and alone in Hell's Kitchen two hundred years ago while waiting for her lover to return. Her nocturnal spirit

plagued actress June Havoc out of sleep for years, and not even the best psychics could ease Lucy's endless torment. Then there is the ghost of Alexander Hamilton, who stalks the environs of Jane Street, where his earthly body breathed last, having been shot in a duel by his mortal enemy, Aaron Burr. Is it justice he seeks? A redress for the harm done to him? Or just understanding? It is

interesting that Burr himself also continues to haunt the city, in a modern-day restaurant that was once his carriage house.

But it is not only those cursed in life who roam modern New York. There are others whose spirit has been so entwined in the city during life that they seem to prefer to stay here in death. Ghosts such as Peter Stuyvesant, the first governor of New

Above: New York City as seen at night, when its spirits and ghosts walk abroad. The "city that never sleeps" is apparently just as much an attraction for restless souls as it is for the living who come looking for excitement.

Above: Welsh poet Dylan Thomas pictured the White Horse Tavern, the scene of his last drinking binge. In the dead of night, his ghost creeps back to sit at the table where once he wrote.

Amsterdam, who watched over the settlement as a father in life and walks the streets even now, dutifully watching even in death. Or Gertrude Tredwell, who lived for almost a century in what is now Merchant's House Museum on East Fourth Street. During that time her entire world of filial obedience and disappointed love was contained within these four walls, and she remains there still, chilling tour guides and visitors with unexplainable manifestations and even personal appearances.

Indeed, the overwhelming majority of hauntings are benign. It could be that the confused spirits that remain after death are unable to navigate their way to whatever the afterlife holds, or that they remain curious to see what human enterprise will bring from the future. Perhaps they are merely comfortable in their surroundings. For example, the legendary Welsh poet Dylan Thomas still returns to the White Horse Tavern, having been one of its best customers back in the 1950s. Thomas died after a marathon drinking spree there, and today his ghost drops by to ensure the table at which he used to write is positioned just so.

In one or two instances, however, there are reports of malignant phenomena that defy explanation, even by the loose terms of what paranormal investigators think of as a typical haunting. One such example may have prompted Mark Twain to write "A Ghost Story." For it is in a house that was once his home that Jan Bartell encountered a truly terrifying presence. This unnamed and unknown entity permeated her house and life with an atmosphere of oppressive evil and dread, walking with heavy feet at night, crashing through the house, and manifesting in a wispy figure that darted through the corridors. In a book she eventually wrote about her experiences, Jan blamed the ghost—if a ghost it was—for twenty-two deaths. A short while after finally fleeing the building, Jan herself died.

A common perception is that ghosts are to be found in desolate, far-flung locations where visitors are rare. The literary and cinematography cliché is that they inhabit old mansions and buildings hidden away behind high walls or barred gates that seethe with neglect and decay. Because of these Gothic conventions that have grown up around hauntings, we do not expect ghosts to be found in noisy, dazzling cities like New York. But the truth is very different, as this book proves. For if we delve into the world's most vibrant city, we find that we are rubbing shoulders with ghosts at every turn. It is true they tend to be found in the older buildings or the sites of long-demolished mansions, particularly around Greenwich Village, but this is certainly not always the case. It seems that the dead do not respect literary principles; they simply cling to the places they knew in life, whether that is a crumbling castle or the Empire State Building.

New Yorkers are not known for being prone to flights of fancy. Quite the opposite, they tend to be proud of their realism and skepticism. It's no accident that New Yorkers are famed as "ball breakers." This is a city whose population likes to cut through the flimflam and call it as they see it. Yet many levelheaded witnesses claim to have seen, heard, or felt ghosts. Could they all have been imagining things? Were they simply experiencing tricks of the mind? It hardly seems possible in such a city of realists. So what did they see? Are these strange inhabitants visitations from beyond the grave or proof of an extra, unknown dimension?

Because ghosts and their appearances seem so strongly predicated on emotion, they can never be scientifically studied in a laboratory environment. And, in response to skeptics who say that those who experience ghostly phenomena are gullible people who want to see ghosts or are desperately searching for an affirmation of life after death, the evidence strongly points in the opposite direction. The vast majority of spectral appearances are witnessed by people who are least expecting them.

Above: Greenwich Village in the early twentieth century. Not always as fashionable as it is now, the Village is the home of a disproportionate amount of New York's ghosts.

Ironically, the more you want to see a ghost, the less likely it is to happen.

More and more people are prepared to accept the existence of ghosts. One poll revealed that belief in them has increased from 25 percent to 38 percent in the last ten years. That's quite a leap of faith. For even if we are convinced that ghosts exist, we are still far from understanding the mystery of why, how, and where. Our era may appear on the surface to be less spiritual that ever, but it seems that we are more open than ever to the question of what lies beyond death.

With so many unexplained happenings and phenomena, it would be unwise to discount the existence of ghosts. For every obvious hoax there is another story that will defy explanation from even the most cynical. Surely, not all of the otherwise creditable people who have been witness to New York's strange occurrences can be lying or deluded. And if so, why are their stories so often corroborated by independent witnesses?

Because we reject the things we can't explain, we may often discount a true ghost experience, even when the evidence is overwhelming. So, for all those who have never seen one—and who still don't believe in them—we must trust that the following stories of some of New York City's most colorful ghosts will simply be enjoyed as a part of the folklore of America's most fascinating city. And trust that it might open your mind a bit; after all, can science really understand all there is to know about life and death?

For those whose minds are already open to the possibility of the spirits of the dead remaining, we hope that these stories guide you to some places you might never have visited.

The stories contained in this book have been selected for a number of reasons. Some ghosts, such as Dorothy Parker, are of New York's most illustrious denizens and were chosen because they are so much a part of New York's mystique. Others, like Jan Bartell's tale, were chosen because the accounts are genuinely hair-raising. A few were chosen because of their historical interest. All, however, show that where there is life and death there are restless spirits. Spirits who yearn to reach out and touch the living in any way they can to prove their continued existence. Not even amid the neon and sparkling glass towers of New York are you safe from the sinister attentions of those who should, by all rights, be resting in their graves.

If, on your travels through New York, you happen to meet the shade of Dylan Thomas at the White Horse Tavern, Henrietta Chumley at Chumley's, or the Wraith of the Waverley Inn, buy them a drink and ask them to tell you their tales. At the very least, you'll hear some interesting stories about the world's greatest city.

manhattan and new york city

manhattan and new york city

When considering where and how things happened in New York City, the first

thing to remember is that everything started down at the tip of the island, at

today's Battery Park. This is where the Dutch founded the city of New

Amsterdam in 1624. From that point, the city's history is a constant move

north, up the island. Originally New York City was only Manhattan, but as the

centuries have progressed, so the spread of the Big Apple has gone beyond the

island's boundaries.

It's difficult today for people to imagine any part of New York City as undeveloped, since it's one of the most populated, densely built cities in the world. But the fledgling city was very small; the city limits of Dutch New Amsterdam ended at Wall Street. Even by the time of the American Revolution, the development had only made it up to today's City Hall (originally built in 1812). The rest of the island was farmland, with little settlements dotted here and there. Some of those early settlements, like Harlem, survive as neighborhoods. Other neighborhoods, like Greenwich Village, Chelsea, and Hell's Kitchen, appeared later.

The ghost sites in this book are loosely arranged in geographical order—south to north—starting with St. Paul's Chapel on lower Broadway and proceeding up Manhattan toward the Morris-Jumel Mansion in the city's northern sector. There's also a visit to Staten Island, where the Old Bermuda Inn is haunted by a lovely lady ghost still waiting for her husband to return from the Civil War.

In selecting stories for this book, the focus has been on some of New York City's most colorful spirits and intriguing locations—places that are easy to find and visit. Though some, such as Melrose Hall, have become victims of road-widening schemes and the march of progress, there are many that can still be visited. Quite a few of the tales revolve around Greenwich Village. Whether it is the concentration of old houses there or Village residents' willingness to talk about their ghosts, it does seem like there are more haunted spots here than in any other neighborhood. But these are certainly not all the ghosts of New York—not by a long shot. There are at least forty-eight well-known locations in Manhattan alone, and several of them boast multiple ghosts.

Every Halloween, one city or another proclaims itself "the most haunted city in America," but it's doubtful that any other place can equal the sheer volume of paranormal activity occurring daily in New York City. Maybe these ghosts draw upon the city's energy. Or maybe New York is just such a great place that many don't want to leave—not even when they're dead.

Below: New York circa 1873. Battery Park, in the foreground, is the oldest part of the city and full of ghostly tales.

the headless ghost of st. paul's

churchyard st. paul's chapel—broadway at fulton street

At Broadway on Fulton Street, St. Paul's is New York's oldest surviving church.

Around it lie the graves of Revolutionary War heroes, distinguished New

Yorkers, and one anomaly—the city's first superstar actor. An Englishman.

Unlike his American neighbors in so many ways, the spirit of George

Frederick Cooke does not lie in peace. Over the last two centuries, while

Manhattan has risen all around the old church, his specter has also risen from

the grave, stalking among the tombstones and grave markings. Is it possible .

that in death Cooke continues to crave the attention of an audience?

Mystery surrounds the removal of Cooke's skull, but while his shade appears to occasional nighttime passersby in the cemetery of St. Paul's, his physical remains were at one time seen by thousands. Soon after his demise, the skull of this turbulent actor somehow made its way back to the theater, to be lifted aloft by actor after actor, always accompanied by the words "Alas, poor Yorick. I knew him, Horatio: a fellow of infinite jest . . ."

Cooke was always a difficult man. He was endowed with phenomenal talent, and his performances set eighteenth-century England ablaze. Even during his descent into the despairing alcoholism that would ultimately spell his end, his natural ability never truly deserted him. Eventually, though, the audiences of his native country grew weary of his erratic acting and the frequent apologies of the stage manager as the curtain was pulled. That was if Cooke had turned up at all. As one playful manager reported to spectators, "Mr. Cooke has a bowl condition," alluding to the bowl of punch that had taken the actor's senses yet again.

A drunk, a womanizer, and a persona non grata on the British stage, the road that would lead to persons unknown dismembering the actor's corpse began in

Opposite: Built in 1764, St. Paul's is a chapel of Trinity, and is the oldest house of worship in Manhattan. It bears the distinction of having had President George Washington among its worshippers during the brief period that New York City was the nation's first capital. Washington's pew is suitably marked within the church. This photograph was taken in 1959.

Left: In the colonial period, and for years thereafter, most American churches had surrounding graveyards. The ancient, predominantly brownstone, markers at St. Paul's bear witness to the many years of history the beautiful old chapel has witnessed.

1810. In that year Cooke accepted the offer of a series of guest appearances in the New World. With his career in tatters and poverty beckoning, he had little choice.

At first, all seemed to go well. The long voyage and the prospect of a fresh start agreed with Cooke's health, and he reprised many of his most famous roles to a rapturous American crowd. Eager audiences camped overnight outside Manhattan's Park Theatre to secure tickets. He played Iago in *Othello*, Falstaff in *Henry IV*, and—to great acclaim—Richard III. It was not long, however, before the temptations of a life given over to debauchery reclaimed him. Soon the same disapproving reviews as had appeared back in England began to be seen in the New York press. Cooke had failed to appear on stage. When he did he stumbled over his words and fellow actors. Incredibly, his audiences

were forgiving and Cooke's first season in New York was hailed a success. He was welcomed back with open arms following his tours of Boston, Philadelphia, and Richmond, Virginia, and enjoyed two more successful seasons at the Park Theatre in 1811 and 1812.

Away from the limelight, though, Cooke's health was deteriorating and the actor, now in his late fifties or early sixties (depending on which account of his life you read), slowly spiraled toward death. He was nursed by either his third or fifth wife: again the facts are confused, like so much else in the life of a man committed to excess.

At six o'clock in the morning of September 26, 1812, as the sun rose, the grave finally claimed him. But if anyone thought the well-attended funeral was the final curtain for George Frederick Cooke, they were mistaken. Before long, tales began to circulate of a terrifying figure moving around the churchyard at night, appearing and vanishing in the blink of an eye. It was said that the figure was of a man without a head.

Initially laid to rest in the strangers' vault, Cooke's body was later moved to a more prominent position in the center of the churchyard at the insistence of fellow actor and countryman Edmund Kean, who also funded an elaborate marble monument, comprising a column topped with a flaming urn. When it was found that at some point the actor's head had been removed, the answer to the mystery of the headless specter in the cemetery seemed obvious. Cooke's spirit was pitifully searching for his lost skull.

How and why the body and head came to be separated remains unknown, but it is certain that at some point unrecorded, the latter began to make a guest appearance in the famous gravedigger's scene in Shakespeare's *Hamlet*.

If supernatural agencies are discounted, then one plausible theory has it that the actor pledged his head to science in lieu of paying his doctor's bills. But if this was so, how did his skull come to appear once again on the stage while his shade walked the night across Broadway? A fact that gives credence to some semblance of this theory is that Cooke's skull was finally given to the Jefferson Medical School in Philadelphia by Dr. Valentine Mott Francis, son of Dr. John

Francis, one of Cooke's physicians during his dying days. It is possible that Cooke's doctor, obeying his client's dying wishes, removed his head for science as agreed and, after it had been dissected and experimented on, the remaining skull was loaned to the theater.

Another explanation would be that Cooke, forever arrogant in life, wished for his career to go on after death and planned the brutal dismemberment of his own corpse in order that some part of him might continue to be lit up in the footlights. Certainly this would be typical of the mercurial and disturbed actor.

The only other possible route from the grave to the stage would be that some person or persons unknown crept into the stranger's vault of St. Paul's and stole the corpse's head. Could it be that Cooke was the victim of some grisly theatrical prank?

Whatever strange events took place following Cooke's death, it is said that the headless actor can still occasionally be seen among the tastefully restrained grave markers around an elegant church in a land far away from his home. Even in death, Cooke receives the recognition he always felt was rightly his. For no one could ever mistake his ghostly appearance—even without the head he tossed so arrogantly in life. Despite several proposals, the skull has never been reunited with Cooke's body in St. Paul's churchyard. Perhaps if it was, New York would finally lose one of its most dramatic ghosts.

Above: Walking around the fenced-in churchyard can give you the shivers. And well it should, because this old burial ground is home to a specter dressed in the clothes of an early nineteenth-century gentleman, wandering among the shadows of the ancient tombstones in constant search for the one thing he obviously lacks—his head!

waiting for his ship to come in

ear inn—326 spring street

There are many reports of the lingering of spirits of those who died sudden,

unexpected deaths. It would appear that these unfortunate souls, who have life

taken from them so quickly and arbitrarily, are unwilling or unable to move on

to whatever the afterlife holds. Instead, they cling to the places they knew in

life, their existence slight and insubstantial but just tangible enough to make

their presence felt and, occasionally, strike terror into the living. One such

ghost is that of Mickey the Sailor. The tavern rooms he once settled in are now

apartments, but the dead seaman still considers them home. And his spirit

manifests itself in a particularly chilling way to the women who live there.

On one of New York's most haunted streets is a famous old bar, known as the Ear Inn for the last four decades. Previously, however—during the Prohibition years—it was known as the Green Door. Dim, warm, and with a cavalier attitude to the Draconian drinking laws, it was popular among sailors who put ashore at the thriving docks on the nearby Hudson River. While awaiting their next voyage, they could come here for a hot meal and to drink illegal liquor, then climb the hostelry's stairs to sleep off the alcohol in one of the upstairs rooms. Even then it was an old place, built in 1817 for its first owner, a free African American named James Brown who served in the Revolution as aide-de-camp to General Washington. Over the years since it became a tavern, the bar downstairs hasn't changed much apart from its name. Indeed, it was granted landmark status in 1970 by the New York Preservation Commission. Upstairs, though, the rooms once used by sailors are now residential apartments. Nevertheless, one of the Green Door's best customers remains.

Mickey the Sailor was, as his name suggests, a mariner during his working life, and when the time came for him to retire, he

Opposite: Despite its changes of name over the past two centuries, this building by the Hudson River, now known as the Ear Inn, still draws a weary soul to its bar. We know him only by the name Mickey the Sailor. He was retired and lived in one of the rooms above the tavern. One day he walked out into the street and was run over and killed. Since then, Mickey has been haunting the bar and the upstairs living quarters.

took a room at the Green Door. Here he could eat, drink, and enjoy the company of other seafarers as he had been used to all his life, while taking a well-deserved rest in the twilight of his years.

No one knows if it was pure accident or whether Mickey was the worse for drink, but upon stepping out into the street one day, he was run down and killed by a motorist. Whoever was to blame, the result was the same. Mickey passed from life to death almost instantaneously.

It seems that rather than go peacefully into the beyond, Mickey had other ideas.

Over the ensuing years his presence has been felt many times, and the sailor chooses to manifest himself in one way that is particularly unsettling to those who witness the visitation. Above the bar, in the apartments that were once occupied by drunken sailors, women who thought themselves safe and warm in their beds have reported awaking in the night convinced that a male presence was in the room. Some say that this presence has even attempted to get into bed with them. Terrified as only those at their most vulnerable can be, these women have subsequently discovered no living

Left: This photograph was taken shortly before Thomas Cloke sold the place at the onset of Prohibition. It then became a popular sailor's hangout, the Green Door, and operated as a speakeasy, with a restaurant in the front and illegal liquor sales taking place behind a curtain in the back room. The building's entire facade was painted green, and there are still traces of green paint on the brick face of the house.

person in the room, but the feeling of a man being there is unshakable.

If only one or two instances had been reported, then perhaps these events could be put down to particularly vivid nightmares, but Mickey, it seems, is persistent and the tales are too similar to be discounted simply as the products of unconscious minds. Perhaps his ghost is merely confused. It could be that having been taken so swiftly from life,

the mariner's shadow is merely repeating his daily routine—after all, these were the rooms in which he slept, and what could be more natural than getting into your own bed? The alternative is the spine-tingling thought that even in death the sailor still has an eye for the ladies, and, no longer able to have a girl in every port, he patiently waits in his old familiar rooms, killing time until the women come to him.

ghosts of old st. patrick's

OLD ST. PATRICK'S CATHEDRAL—MOTT STREET BETWEEN PRINCE AND HOUSTON

High in the Gothic vaults, whispers are sometimes heard, and out in the

graveyard strange mist formations have been reported as the night closes in.

Are these simple windblown fall fogs, or—as witnesses say—are the ghosts of

Old St. Patrick's unwilling to leave their spiritual home? Certainly, such mists as

have been seen outside the old church are well known to paranormal

investigators, who refer to the phenomenon as "ectoplasm." As with anything

related to supernatural research, there is much argument about what

ectoplasm is, but many believe that it is the manifestation of spiritual energy:

literally, the vestiges of the dead.

Old and Gothic, St. Patrick's has presided over Little Italy for nearly two hundred years. The old church was once the heart of the archdiocese of New York, from its consecration in 1815 to the opening of the new St. Patrick's on Fifth Avenue in 1987. Over that time, it has given spiritual comfort to untold thousands and provided a final resting place for bishops and simple New Yorkers alike. Not all of them, it seems, are ready to depart. Tales of hauntings abound at St. Patrick's.

Perhaps the most well known of the church's ghosts is that of Bishop John DuBois. The bishop passed away on December 20, 1842, but before he did so he was moved to decree that when he died, he wanted to be buried beneath the entrance to the cathedral. His reason, he asserted, was that "People have walked all over me in life, so they might as well do the same when I am dead." It is true that the bishop was no stranger to trouble in his lifetime; the trustees of the cathedral once even threatened to stop his wages over a financial dispute.

At the beginning of the twentieth century, diocese officials decided to take an "inventory" of clergy buried in the

Left: When the old cathedral was begun in 1809, New York's Roman Catholic community was relatively small, but there were already enough Irish immigrants here to ensure that the new church was named after Ireland's patron saint. Old St. Patrick's still stands on Mott Street, surrounded by its picturesque graveyard. It is rich in history—and ghosts.

underground crypt. All were accounted for—except Bishop John DuBois. Remembering the old—and odd—legend that the bishop had requested to be buried beneath the entrance, digging began under the flagstones in front of the church door. The searchers eventually unearthed the remains of the bishop, and a new memorial was erected over the spot. Nevertheless, the bishop has spent very little time resting under the door, for his recognizable form is the most frequently seen in the church and the surrounding graveyard. Why he stays is a mystery, but while alive the bishop was full of zeal for his church and his flock. It is possible that in death he wishes to remain to keep a watchful eye over his successors and his parishioners.

The bishop is in good company. Another spirit, who has been seen wringing his hands or whispering a prayer, is that of Pierre Toussaint, a freed slave whose piety and goodness in life led to him being considered for sainthood in the 1990s. In preparation for the event, his physical remains were disinterred and moved to the more prestigious surroundings of the crypt beneath the new St. Patrick's. Perhaps the humble Toussaint wishes to return to his final resting place, to be closer to his wife and their adopted daughter.

The area around the cathedral in the nineteenth century was so deprived that Charles Dickens, on visiting in the 1840s, was moved to comment that the area was on a par with London's great slums that he depicted in *Oliver Twist* and other tales. The majority of the population were Irish folk who had fled from the potato famine in their native country to start a new life here. Instead they found poverty, prejudice, and, in the Civil War, a conflict that they felt was not their concern. Such was the anti-Irish, anti-Catholic sentiment that this provoked that it is said that the wall around St. Patrick's was raised to protect the building and those who sheltered there. Public feeling against the draft eventually erupted in the violence of the draft riots, during which various estimates put the number of dead at anywhere between seventy and a thousand. Are the wispy figures seen floating through the south graveyard the ghosts of those poor folk who died, malnourished in the filthy streets or persecuted in the political unrest?

There are yet more, recent examples of spiritual activity at St. Patrick's. Among the church's official engagements was a 1999 televised memorial service for John F. Kennedy Jr. In some of the footage from the event, it is possible to make out a wispy clerical figure who is clearly not of the mourning party.

While a few of Old St. Patrick's ghosts are reported to be recognizable apparitions, many are of wisps: mistlike shapes that paranormal investigators call ectoplasm. They appear in and outside of the church. There is no easy explanation why—if eyewitnesses are to be believed—so many

Left: The new grave marker of Bishop DuBois, at the doorway of St. Patrick's. Most people walking by the cathedral don't realize that another burial ground exists beneath the churchyard—in the underground vault. Within the crypt below the church, which even extends under Mott Street, prominent Catholic citizens are buried.

Opposite: This photograph, taken in 1888, shows the Five Points slums that were home to New York's Irish immigrants. The neighborhood was known as the Five Points because of its five intersecting streets. Because it offered cheap housing and cheaper amusements to the poor and the newly arrived immigrants, by the mid-nineteenth century the Five Points had become the city's worst slum and was notorious throughout America.

spirits would wish to linger here. Many churches are just as old yet are completely undisturbed by paranormal activity. Bishop DuBois, while devoted to his church and his flock, does not appear to have been more so than any number of other bishops who have left this world peacefully behind. If the once-desperate conditions of its parishioners are responsible for the hauntings, then why are there not more reports of ghostly hands clutching at the pockets of passersby in what was once Dickensian London?

Of course, it is impossible to answer such questions, but the fact remains that Old St. Patrick's appears to be unusually over-populated with specters, wraiths, and ectoplasmic manifestations.

just Like papa would have wanted
merchant's house museum—29 east fourth street

To some, death makes very little difference. It merely marks a transition from

one plane of existence to another. Gertrude Tredwell is just such an example.

For ninety-three years—from the cradle to the grave—she lived a shadowy life

in her family home at 29 East Fourth Street, and the demise of her physical

body has proved no obstacle to her continuing to do so. For almost a century,

everything she was ever allowed to love was contained within these four walls,

an entire lifetime of caring and dusting and polishing and making sure that

everything was kept as neat and tidy as it had always been. Outside, the world

moved on, changing out of all recognition, but within the house time has been

caught like a fly in amber. And Gertrude's soul is trapped with it.

The prosperous Tredwell family moved into the handsome, Federal-style house in 1840, and Gertrude, the last of eight children, was born here soon after. Little did the family know that their beautiful youngest daughter would continue to haunt the place into the twenty-first century. The family's remaining possessions—photographs, theater programs, holiday souvenirs, and the like—provide evidence of a happy family given to entertainment while devoted to the Episcopal Church. However, there are few documents that offer any deeper insight into their lives, and any secrets that the family had are shrouded by time. As far as we know, Eliza and Seabury Tredwell had all that any parents of their time could wish for: a comfortable living in an elegant part of town and fine sons and daughters who would be assured eligible matches.

But they were to be disappointed. The two boys and two eldest daughters did marry, but then disaster struck another of the girls. Sarah was involved in a carriage

Opposite: The Merchant's House, located half a block off Lafayette Street in the East Village. This wonderfully preserved house, now a museum open to the public, has come down to us like a time capsule, thanks to Gertrude Tredwell, whose spirit still dwells within her home of ninety-three earthly years.

Left: The master bedroom, where Gertrude died in 1933. Over the years since the house was opened as a museum, staff members and visitors alike have had encounters with Gertrude's ghost. Many of the employees have told stories of experiencing cold spots in the house. Other staff members have told of stepping out onto the roof on a windless day and having the door slammed behind them. Often, indentations are seen in the beds in the two upstairs master bedrooms, as though someone had just arisen after an afternoon nap.

accident and was forced to stay at home as an invalid. The next two daughters simply failed to find suitors.

The last of their children was to become the most disenchanted. Pretty young Gertrude fell passionately in love in her early twenties. The young man in question was all she had ever dreamed of, and as a medical student seemed perfectly acceptable, except for one thing: his Catholicism. Gertrude's devoutly Episcopal father would not hear of the marriage, and in those times his despairing daughter had no choice but to follow his wishes and watch her life's happiness crumble into dust. She was never to find another man she could love so well, and instead of finding the joy of her own family, she slipped into a quiet and dutiful spinsterhood.

After their mother passed away, Gertrude and her sisters remained in their childhood home, while the neighborhood changed radically around them. In the post–Civil War period, the East Fourth Street area ceased being fashionable, or even residential. It became commercial in the 1880s and 1890s, when many of the old townhouses were torn down and replaced by warehouses and factories. During Gertrude's life, little was done to modernize the house, except for the addition of electric lighting and indoor plumbing.

In these surroundings, which were slowly slipping into a bygone era, Gertrude's sisters died one by one, and finally only she was left, living alone with a hired companion and keeping her house, as she said, "the way Papa would have wanted." In 1933 Gertrude died at age ninety-three in the master bedroom, which had originally been her father's, leaving behind a remarkable monument to a lost age—and her spirit.

George Chapman, a distant cousin of the Tredwells, could not believe his eyes when he first walked into the place. Dusty but in remarkably good condition, the furniture and all the fittings were from the previous century. Although Gertrude had allowed electricity to be installed, she had insisted on retaining the original chandeliers and oil-burning lights. All the family's possessions spoke of years long gone.

Chapman was quick to recognize the historical worth of the house and quickly moved to open it as a museum. He ensured that all modern restoration in the house was done with authentic materials to replicate the original curtains, bed canopies, and carpets. Perhaps by doing so he helped ensure Gertrude's continued presence. If the house had been renovated and redecorated in a more modern style, perhaps her spirit would have acknowledged that she was no longer a part of the building. Since the museum is a perfect restoration of the

Tredwell home, we will never know.

Gertrude Tredwell refuses to leave the Merchant's House. Museum staff are used to her presence and simply shiver in the frequent, unexplainable cold spots of the building instead of running away. Such spots are well-known indicators of paranormal activity, and some investigators suggest that they result from a ghost's drawing energy from its surroundings as it materializes, causing the temperature to drop. However they are caused, such spots are disconcerting. One witness describes the experience as "like standing under an air-conditioning vent—only the house isn't air-conditioned."

Other staff members tell stories of how doors slam when there is no wind to blow them and of indentations that appear in the beds in the two upstairs master bedrooms—one of which, of course, was the room where Gertrude spent her last hours in this life.

Another spiritual phenomenon that is familiar to paranormal investigators are known as "orbs." These strange, glowing balls that appear on camera are said to be the light of spirit energy. If this is so, it explains why a bright, glowing sphere mysteriously appeared in the center of a photograph of a group of bridesmaids taken in an upstairs room. For those who knew the story of Gertrude's own unrealized marriage, it is eerie that the only time this phenomenon has been observed at the house was during a day that it had been rented out to a

wedding party. Is this a manifestation of a bitter woman, or could it be that Gertrude merely wants to be part of the festivities she was denied during life? Whatever the reason, it is compelling that such evidence of a presence would show up so clearly when there was a wedding in the house.

Sometimes, though, Gertrude is even bolder. One visitor to the museum tells of how the front door was opened by a sad young woman dressed in a brown silk costume that belonged to a period long gone. "She shook her head and told me the house was not open," he said. "She told me to come back another time."

When he did return a few days later, no one could throw any light on exactly who the woman was: none of the staff matched his description, and none wore period costume. Perplexed, the visitor began his tour of the

house, only to find a familiar face looking out at him from an old photograph. The person who opened the door to him was Gertrude.

Stories such as this are rightly treated with skepticism; it is likely that many are hoaxes. In this case, however, the visitor described the dress that "Gertrude" wore very clearly. Although it was not on display at the time, a dress exactly matching his description does exist in the museum's collection and at one time belonged to one of the Tredwell sisters. How this visitor to the museum could have known or guessed about it remains unexplained.

Today, as people walk through that long, narrow hall, slip through the huge mahogany doors that divide the formal parlors, or marvel at the beautifully retained brick-lined beehive oven, they can be assured that, although perhaps on their own, they are certainly not alone. Gertrude's spirit remains, wistfully haunting her old home, perhaps still grieving for her lost life and love, or maybe just so much a part of the house that she cannot bring herself to leave it. For nearly two hundred years she has existed within the same four walls, having seen so little of life that maybe she cannot find the courage to find what death has in store for her.

Left: The photograph of Gertrude from which a visitor was able to identify the young woman who opened the door to him. Gertrude's appearances bring up an interesting point about ghosts. Are they "suspended" in a particular time period? Do they choose how they look when they appear to the living? Gertrude is always seen as a young woman in her twenties, but we know that she was ninety-three years old when she died. Is her ghost forever fixed in a parallel time—perhaps the happiest time in her life, when she was being courted by the young medical student?

the governor's watchful eye

the GOVERNOR'S watchful eye

st. mark's in the Bowery—131 east tenth street

After losing a leg in battle, Peter Stuyvesant, New York's first governor, was

fitted with a wooden one. Banded with silver, it made his approach

unmistakable: a footstep followed by the tap of metal, as regular as his

measured pace. Today, even the most skeptical would find it a very odd

coincidence that this sound can still be heard at St. Mark's in the Bowery,

where the governor's old bones are entombed. Some believe that the old

tyrant is so passionate about his city that he stays to keep watch over it. There

are even reports that now, more than at any other time in memory, the tap,

tap, tap of his passage can be heard. What could have stirred him even further

from his slumber? Could it be that he senses danger to his beloved city?

Any New York schoolchild can recite the story of Peter Stuyvesant, the benevolent yet stern governor of New Amsterdam, dispatched by the Dutch West India Company over three and a half centuries ago to turn the settlement into a prosperous trading port. In *Knickerbocker's History of New York*, Washington Irving calls him a "tough, sturdy, valiant, weather-beaten, mettlesome, obstinate, leathern-sided, lion-hearted, generous-spirited old governor," and he brought all these qualities

to his rule over what he thought of as "his children." He watched over the colony as a strict father would, from his appointment in 1647 until 1664, when a British war fleet arrived and the anguished governor saw his beloved New Amsterdam become New York.

Stuyvesant subsequently retired to his vast "bouwerie" (the Dutch word for farm). The street that today we call the Bowery was originally the road from the city of New Amsterdam (way downtown) to Stuyvesant's bouwerie. Here he continued to watch over

the rapidly growing city until his death in 1880, at which time he was interred in the family crypt beneath the chapel that he had commissioned. Death, however, was simply another challenge to the strong-willed old soldier. A challenge that could be overcome if he was provoked.

A century later, the chapel was torn down and replaced with the church that now stands on the site. After the building was finished, puzzled visitors and worshippers began to talk about the strange tapping noise that could be heard from time to time. No one could understand what produced this sound—until the ethereal apparition of a stern-looking man in colonial costume was seen in the graveyard. The man appeared to have a

Left: Following the arrival of the British, Stuyvesant retired to his bouwerie in the country, where he lived until his death in 1672. He was buried in the crypt of the family chapel, which stood on the farm property. The family chapel was torn down and replaced by a new Episcopal church, St. Mark's in the Bowery, built in 1799. Today near the busy intersection of Second Avenue and East Tenth Street, St. Mark's remains Manhattan's second-oldest church building, built over the Stuyvesant family burial vault. In the old churchyard, beneath its ancient elm trees, are the graves of some of New York's elite.

wooden leg. The answer to the mystery, it seemed, lay in the crypt. Its most famous resident was no longer resting.

But why is old Peter not content to remain with his descendants? It is suggested that he was disturbed by the leveling of his old chapel and the building work that followed. More likely, though, is that he watches over the city in death as he did in life. In 1978, when St. Mark's suffered a disastrous fire, which destroyed the roof and gutted a large part of its interior, the fire department arrived to hear the steeple bell furiously clanging. It was assumed that someone inside was ringing the alarm, though no one came forward. Soon after, the firefighters found that the bell's rope had burned so far above the ground that no human could have made it ring. Most give old Governor Stuyvesant credit for sounding the alarm, but if he was upset about the loss of his chapel, why would he stir himself to save its replacement?

Like all of the ghost stories in this book, there are enough reports of paranormal activity around St. Mark's to lend credence to the stories. It would stretch belief to think that every one of the tales was a hoax; indeed, many have come from the church's flock. But if we are to believe that Governor Stuyvesant is watching over his property from beyond the grave, why has his appearance become so frequent now? His is a popular ghost tale, and one that is repeated with amusement. But perhaps the old governor's spirit is dismissed too easily. It could be that the tapping of his wooden leg spells out danger to New Amsterdam.

the HAUNTED speakeasy

CHUMLeY's—86 BeDford street

Henrietta Chumley lost her life as she had lost her consciousness night after night, slumped across her usual table by the fire. When the waitstaff went to carry her home—as they did at the end of every day—they found that the years of heavy drinking and smoking had finally killed her. Not that Henrietta would allow a little thing like death to prevent her keeping the bar just as she wanted it. A matriarch in death as she was in life, Henrietta reminds staff and customers of her presence whenever change is threatened. Bottles come crashing down, unexplained noises are heard, and anything that smacks of modern technology will not work. Thus Mrs. Chumley maintains the authentic atmosphere at New York's most difficult-to-find speakeasy.

While some ghosts are connected to their haunts by tragic events or unresolved circumstances, there are others that linger because they seem to prefer their surroundings to whatever death has in store for them. Mrs. Chumley is the unquestioned proprietor of Chumley's bar now as she was in life, but hers is not a story of emotional anguish or bloody murder. She simply views the bar as her "patch," and such is the power of her personality that no one has had the courage to argue with her.

In her day, Henrietta Chumley was something of an enigma. She first stepped through the door of Chumley's soon after the death of Lee Chumley and announced that she was taking over the reins of her husband's business. Not that this was particularly strange, even in the 1930s, and besides, Chumley's had never been an orthodox business. What was odd, though, was that in all the years that he had run the bar, through its days as an illegal drinking den through the repeal of Prohibition, Lee

Opposite: Bedford Street in Greenwich Village hid a a little 1831 brick-front Federal-style house, at number 86, between Grove and Barrow. Covered on the front with stucco, it had a metal grill on the front door to make it look like a garage. Behind this door was a cozy little speakeasy that remains there still, complete with the ghost of its original owner's wife.

Chumley had never mentioned having a wife. Perhaps he liked to keep his business and private lives separate. Perhaps it was a deliberate tactic to keep any police investigation away from his wife. Or perhaps Mrs. Chumley was just a grifter whose criminal eye recognized that staff at the shady bar probably wouldn't ask too many questions and that here was a business opportunity that would set her up for life.

With access only through an unmarked door at the end of a hidden courtyard, Pamela Court, Chumley's was, in its day, the ultimate speakeasy. Some said it was the hardest place to find in New York. The cunningly disguised front door was for emergencies only: for a quick escape when the place got raided, which happened at least three times during those Prohibition days. Indeed, the Bedford front door still bears the number 86, which gave rise to the slang expression "86 it" when the Feds came to call through the back of Chumley's.

If she was indeed an opportunist, Henrietta Chumley knew her business: the staff was pleased to have a hand at the rudder again, and Henrietta was soon comfortably enthroned at her seat by the fire as an absolute matriarch. Her lackeys soon found out, though, that one thing she despised more than anything else was change. This is why she sat at her regular table with her regular drink, smoking endlessly, night after night, year after year. And why, while all around other bars were renovated, redecorated, and revamped, Henrietta's place remained the same sawdust-on-the-floor establishment it had been as a speakeasy. Although the bar was now legal, she wouldn't even allow a sign put up (there is none still, and Chumley's remains the most difficult establishment in New York to find). After all, if the place was good enough as it was for the likes of Ernest Hemingway, William

Left (above and below): Novelist F. Scott Fitzgerald and poet Edna St. Vincent Millay were regular patrons at Chumley's. Perhaps because of its homey atmosphere, the bar drew many of the young creative people, especially writers, who had moved to Greenwich Village in the 1920s. Regular customers also included Theodore Dreiser and John Dos Passos. But out-of-town literary lights also visited—Faulkner and Hemingway were both occasional Chumley's patrons. They are commemorated today by photos hung on the walls and by the dust jackets of their books, given to Lee Chumley as thanks for his hospitality.

Faulkner, and the great F. Scott Fitzgerald, all of whom dropped by from time to time, then it should be good enough for anyone.

After being found literally dead drunk, Henrietta has become practiced at the art of making her opinions felt from the spirit world. Bottles and glasses fall off shelves if she is displeased, and anything that might bring the bar up-to-date fails to work. Following her death, a pinball machine was installed, but Henrietta made sure no one ever played it, though there was nothing wrong with it mechanically. It was the same story with a CD jukebox. Not one sound could anyone get out of it, and the service engineer was completely flummoxed. As soon as it was removed to other premises, the machine worked fine. On another occasion a crew from a television station visited to tape some footage at Chumley's. Despite several attempts, their equipment just filmed static on the premises. Finally they gave up and took the faulty cameras back to the studio, where they worked just fine as soon as they were unpacked. Maybe, if they had listened very hard to the white noise on the tapes they took away from the bar, they might have been able to hear Mrs. Chumley laughing.

It would appear that Henrietta wants her bar to continue as a secret establishment, exclusive to those in the know: a cozy place for intimate conversation and serious drinking. She doesn't like tours being conducted of her historic old speakeasy; the staff has to apologize on her behalf as bottles come crashing down. But even when things are exactly as she likes, she is careful to remind the staff who's boss and let them know she's keeping an eye on them. Glasses, washed and put away, will reappear on tables when backs are turned, and she still likes to crash and bump around the bar as in the days when she was usually too drunk by the end of the evening to stand on her own.

Below: During Chumley's Prohibition days, customers entered through the unmarked door at the end of the secluded Pamela Court on Barrow Street. The front door was reserved for escapes in case the place got raided.

the ghosts of gay street

12 gay street

As any paranormal investigator will tell you, it is important to keep an open, but skeptical, mind when dealing with a haunting. The most commonplace explanation can be found for some, and more can be rationalized as the fancies of those who may have been duped by their own overactive imaginations or outright hoaxers who like the attention their spooky tales bring. Occasionally, though, two unconnected and trustworthy people will tell the same story of a house at different points in time. And when the second person to have witnessed exactly the same events is unaware of a previous owner's testimony, it becomes very intriguing. Should the story concern not one, but three distinct hauntings, surely there can be no coincidence.

In Europe, where many houses count their histories in centuries rather than decades, multiple hauntings are common. There are less instances to be found in the relatively youthful homes of the United States. However, New York is an old city, and Gay Street can trace its history back nearly two hundred years to the family who once owned this land and gave the street its name. In that time, it seems that three spirits have attached themselves to the house at number twelve. When Frank Paris, the creator of *Howdy Doody*, bought the house in the 1950s, it quickly became clear to him that there was something strange in the house. Paris, a man with no connection to the paranormal before or after his time at Gay Street, began to hear and see things for which he could find no rational explanation. As a last resort, he turned to a medium and a series of séances was held.

The first ghost to be identified was an agonized soul whose utterances were mostly screams and moans. With difficulty it was

Opposite: If you venture down a twisting and turning block-long street just off Sixth Avenue, you may find yourself literally surrounded by ghosts. One charming little house on this street is home to three spirits, each from a different time period. But collectively they're known as the ghosts of Gay Street.

established that this was the spirit of a French diplomat who had been brought to the house early in the nineteenth century and tortured to death under suspicion of spying. (Interestingly, a section of Greenwich Village close by had a thriving French community at this time in history.) Unfortunately, such was the poor man's pain that very little else

could be ascertained about his life or the charges against him.

The second was from the roaring 1920s. Most spirits had a strong connection in life with the place they are haunting, which makes this ghost particularly mysterious. His is the soul of a party guest who won't leave. Dressed in a tuxedo, he appears to have

Above: Number 12 is a typical two-and-a-half-story Federal redbrick with a pitched roof pierced by windows known as "dormers." Behind its unobtrusive facade walk three spirits who for very different reasons are unable to leave the house behind.

visited the house when it belonged to Canadian cabaret singer Betty Compton (it was a present from her lover, New York mayor Jimmy Walker).

The final spirit had a sad tale to tell. A middle-aged man, he is dressed in his best clothes, ready to attend his daughter's wedding. As he was leaving the house, though, he was run down and killed by a passing horse-drawn carriage. His ghost is now seen descending the steps to the street, where it disappears only to rematerialize moments later, to make the fruitless journey over again. Such specters are known to investigators as "repeating ghosts" and seem to be doomed to duplicate their final moments in this world over and over again. Many people have reported seeing this ghost on the street outside number twelve, including the late William Kunstler, a defense attorney and a man most certainly not given to flights of fancy.

Of the two ghosts whose history is clearest, it may be no accident that they died sudden, violent deaths. The party-going spirit was unable to give his reason for staying on at the scene of the party, and research has yet to turn up any useful information, but it is possible that he also may have died here swiftly during a party, perhaps of a sudden heart attack.

During Frank Paris's time at the house, a number of his friends and acquaintances also saw or felt the presence of the three spirits, but even with the evidence of the séance held here, there are many who would say that the ghosts of Gay Street are an elaborate hoax, perpetrated by a man who liked to entertain children.

Perhaps the most compelling aspect of this story then is the testimony of Walter Gibson, author of the *Shadow* radio mysteries, who owned the house in the 1940s. Mr. Gibson did not know the later owner and stayed quiet about his own experiences at the house, afraid that ghostly mumbo jumbo might tarnish his reputation, and half convinced that his mind, so immersed in dark crime thrillers, was simply playing tricks on him. But it emerged during investigations that Mr. Gibson had quietly reported his conviction that 12 Gay Street was haunted by the spirits of a Frenchman in great pain, a man in 1920s costume, and a well-dressed figure who walked down the front steps only to vanish when he reached the street. It seems barely credible that the tales of these two separate inhabitants of the house could have such similar tales to tell. If this is a hoax, it is so elaborate that the participants even kept their relationship to each other secret and somehow managed to get a respected lawyer to recount his own experience at number 12 on television. If we can assume that the most obvious explanation is the most likely, it would appear that despite changing hands many times, the house has three permanent occupants.

tHe mOst HaUNteD Restaurant

tHe mOst HaUNteD Restaurant

IN New YORK ONE IF BY LAND, tWO IF BY sea—17 BARROW stReet

IN New YORK

Dishes smash of their own accord, chairs move from beneath patrons, napkins disappear, and glasses of wine spill. Workmen have seen their tools fly from their boxes and diners have been pushed down stairs. These occurrences sound like scenes from a movie, but such classic poltergeist activity is said to actually happen at New York's most romantic restaurant. Once a carriage house, this building has a history of heartbreak and murder befalling its occupants and owners. Tragedy is at work here; mostly—perhaps—in a place beyond that which the living can see, but occasionally manifesting itself while couples enjoy the wonderful ambience and superb food.

It has been suggested many times that paranormal activity is due to spirits being troubled. Indeed, many of the ghosts in this book are of people who had difficult or tragic lives. Those who have lived and died without regret appear, for the most part, to pass gracefully into whatever death has in store, while those whose lives have been tumultuous are more likely to linger. If this premise holds any truth, then perhaps the more chaotic and turbulent the life, the more violent the soul may become after death. If a haunting can be seen as a kind of emotional barometer, indicating how disturbed is the spirit, then surely the activity of poltergeists must be that of souls in anguish or great fits of passion. To cross the barrier of death and interact with the world of the living must demand energy. While it would be simple for us, the amount of force required for a deceased spirit to tip glasses, lift tools from their boxes, or push people down stairs would be enormous. Is it that what we see is the very tip of the iceberg? Beneath the unexplained tipping of a wineglass might lie a vast reservoir of anger and bitterness, pushing the spirit to

Opposite: In the heart of Greenwich Village is one of the city's most elegant restaurants. One if by Land, Two if by Sea is steeped in New York City history and the paranormal. Enter through the arched doorway and you're in the city's most haunted restaurant.

Left: Most people remember Aaron Burr because of his fateful duel with Alexander Hamilton, which resulted in Hamilton's death and Burr's disgrace, but Burr's story goes far beyond the conflict with Hamilton. Charming, popular with the ladies, and fiercely ambitious, Burr cut a wide swath in both society and politics in America's early years. He was also an important player in New York City's development. Burr owned a large tract of land in Greenwich Village and today's SoHo and eventually purchased Richmond Hill, a pre-Revolutionary mansion located at today's Spring Street and Sixth Avenue.

destructive acts. By the time that anger breaks on the shore of our world, its energy would be so dissipated from the struggle to make itself felt at all that such simple feats would be all that could be achieved. To lift a chair then would be the work of a spirit in great emotional distress or with a huge strength of will.

Such descriptions could both be applied to Aaron Burr, who is said to be the most restless of the ghosts at One if by Land, Two if by Sea. Vice president, victorious duelist, devoted father to a murdered daughter, and a man possessed of great personal charm and fiery ambition, Burr's is a life steeped in the kind of tragedy that could easily lead a soul to disruptive, vengeful action.

Burr is one of history's most enigmatic characters, and to understand how he may have come to haunt a restaurant in the twenty-first century, it is necessary to look back over a life lived at a momentous time in America's history.

A lawyer and politician, Burr made his name in politics during the republic's infancy. Vice president to Thomas Jefferson, he was fiery and opinionated, particularly with his enemies. Like many public figures, however, he had a softer life at home. Following the death of his wife, his pride and joy was a daughter, Theodosia. She was his constant companion and treasured friend. While still a teenager she even played hostess at her father's official functions.

Like all politicians and lawyers, Burr's was a life of verbal conflict and arguments won and lost, but during the course of his career he had earned himself a particularly bitter enemy, Alexander Hamilton. Their long-running feud began with Burr winning the seat of Hamilton's father-in-law and ended with a remark made by Hamilton about Burr at a dinner party and later recorded in the press as a "despicable opinion." It has been whispered that the remark was an allusion to an incestuous liaison between Burr and his daughter, which—incidentally—has no founding whatsoever. All correspondence between father and daughter speaks of a most affectionate and happy relationship.

Although their seconds made all attempts to settle the matter amicably, Hamilton's remark eventually brought him to the dueling ground where he lost his life and Burr his reputation and political career. Indicted for murder in both New York and New Jersey, the winner was forced to flee. During his exile, Burr's creditors confiscated most of his property.

This alone would be enough tragedy for one lifetime, but more was to follow.

Eventually Burr returned to New York to finish his term as vice president, and his beloved daughter married Joseph Alston, a plantation owner from South Carolina. They had a son, whom they named in honor of his grandfather. Frail from birth, the young Aaron Burr Alston died soon after he turned ten. Theodosia was struck down with grief, but again there was worse in store.

Seeking to help his daughter through her time of distress, Burr invited her to stay with him in New York, but on December 31, 1812, her ship, the *Pioneer*, was boarded by pirates. Those aboard were robbed of their possessions and forced to walk the plank to their deaths; Theodosia, wearing a flowing white dress and quietly accepting her fate, was among them. To cover their crime the pirates scuttled the ship, and the deed was only discovered when one of their number was arrested with some of Theodosia's jewelry in his pocket.

What agonies of spirit Burr must have endured can only be imagined. To wonder what had befallen your most beloved when her ship does not arrive, then to believe her perished at sea, only to be faced with worse horror still: cruel murder at the hands of vicious pirates for a handful of trinkets. Such news would have been enough to unhinge the most balanced mind. Even Burr's later wife, Eliza Jumel, could not comfort him.

In an effort to stop his mind from dwelling on the tragedy, all of Theodosia's belongings, and anything else that reminded her father of his daughter, were stored away in the basement of his carriage house, which is now One if by Land, Two if by Sea.

Aaron Burr passed away in 1836 and was duly buried in the President's Lot in Princeton Cemetery. His spirit, however, stayed in New York, close to the earthly belongings of his daughter.

At first his ghost haunted the old stables of his home as well as the old carriage house. His presence here became legendary, even after the building was renovated and became the aptly named Café Bizarre. So much so that in the 1970s a series of séances was held there, during which it is said that Burr was communicative. Another, unrelated séance around this time has deepened the mystery surrounding the uneasy spirits of the Burr family. It has been reported that the first husband of Eliza Jumel claimed from beyond the grave that he was murdered by Burr's future wife. His spirit alleges that he bled to death while his wife watched after she removed the bandages over wounds sustained in a carriage accident.

When Café Bizarre was demolished to make way for a dormitory for the nearby New York University, Burr appears to have deserted the site, and now haunts the restaurant exclusively. Over the years, diners and staff have witnessed many strange events, all of which would seem to adhere to the definition of poltergeist activity. Most paranormal investigators agree that poltergeists are associated with objects moving, rapping noises, and occasionally direct communication. However, they are usually active for short periods of time—a few years at most—and the spirit at One if by Land seems to be an indefinite presence. Its antics would appear at first sight to be almost playful—napkins disappear from customers' laps, their chairs move as they attempt to sit. Small things move of their own volition.

On one occasion, as workmen attended to some rewiring, they turned to see their own tools floating toward them. New York electricians are not renowned as especially easy to scare, but these men would not step into the restaurant again, even though it meant forgoing the pay they were due.

It is not the work of a playful ghost, though, to violently shove customers down the stairs. This dangerous game has been reported a number of times. Various people have spoken of a feeling "like glass or ice" beneath their foot as they place it on a stair, accompanied by the sensation of a push. On other occasions, diners have turned on hearing their names spoken over their shoulder to find the space behind them completely empty.

Left: One if by Land, Two if by Sea is renowned for its romantic atmosphere. The Zagat Restaurant Guide voted it the "most romantic restaurant in New York" and claims that more men have proposed to their future wives here than at any other restaurant in the city. But One if by Land is not only full of charm and fine Continental cuisine—it is full of ghosts.

Those closest to the haunting attest that the most active ghost is that of the former vice president. However, he is not alone. One eyewitness, a former maître d', described what happened late one night as the staff was about to close up after the last Saturday night diner had left. He looked around and saw a female ghost walking down the stairs. She was wearing a long, flowing white dress with a raised Empire-style waist—exactly the fashion in 1812. Could Theodosia be reunited with her father? If so, why would their souls not find some peace?

Yet another ghost is said to haunt the restaurant, an African American man whose identity is unknown. He is sometimes seen on the balcony where the smaller tables are located, but when the waiters go to take his order, he vanishes. Burr had a devoted black valet who worked for him for over thirty years; perhaps it is this man who haunts the restaurant's balcony.

As with so many stories of hauntings, there are many compelling questions but few answers at Burr's old carriage house. How does this spirit manage to interact with material objects so successfully? Why does it do so? Is the "lady in white" Theodosia or some other woman of Burr's era? Is the African American man Burr's manservant? If so, what is his role in these ghostly events? Was Burr's second wife a murderer? It is true that tragedy enough to animate any spirit befell these people, yet could there be some other, darker reason for their haunting what remains of their old property? The answers have all gone to the grave with them. All we can divine now is that Burr is still real enough to tip over a glass of wine or whisper a name in someone's ear.

mark twain's mystery house

There are few tales in this book—or elsewhere—of ghosts that appear to wish serious harm to the living. Some, like Aaron Burr or Mickey the Sailor, may be tricksters, but have done no real injury to anyone. Others, like Gertrude Tredwell, are either passive or helpful. Indeed, most paranormal investigators say that almost without exception the ghosts that they have come across can be classed as "friendly." At 14 and 16 West Tenth Street, though, there is a very different sort of presence, one that has been described as "threatening" and "evil." Many who are familiar with the building hold whatever resides here responsible for numerous deaths. Among the believers was Jan Bartell, who put the number of fatalities at twenty-two in a book she published in 1974. Since then the toll has risen.

Jan Bartell and her husband Fred suffered a particularly chilling "double haunting" during their time in New York from the 1950s through the early 1970s. The locus of their experiences was at 14 West Tenth Street, but before they moved in here the couple lived for a while next door at number 16.

Their first clue that everything about the building was not as it seemed was when their dog started to look at and react to things that the couple could not see. Other unexplained events followed. Rustling noises and the sound of footsteps were heard at night after the lights were turned off. Strange smells, some of them extremely unpleasant and others more like sweet perfume, permeated the apartment. One evening, when Jan was entertaining a friend, there was a crash that sounded like her antique cabinet falling to the floor. Yet when the women rushed to see what damage had been done, the item of

Opposite: Of all the purportedly haunted houses in New York City, none is more mysterious than 14 West Tenth Street, where author Samuel Clemens, better known as Mark Twain, lived in 1900–1901. The house was built in 1854 and is located on one of the most beautiful streets in Greenwich Village, between Fifth and Sixth Avenues.

Left: When Jan Bartell questioned tenants about the house's history, a former super told her that there were stories that Mark Twain's ghost had been seen back in the 1930s. While no such reports have been heard since, it is possible that the writer experienced something of the house's malevolent atmosphere. It would explain his quick departure from the house.

furniture was standing unscathed in its normal place. On another occasion, the Bartells' cleaning lady was paralyzed with fear when a wispy shape floated through the hall. So disturbed was the woman that she quit her job.

But the most frightening thing at number 16 was the overall atmosphere. The building was permeated by a sense of dread, an oppressive feeling that something evil dwelled here, watching and ready.

As a last resort, to try to exorcise whatever was causing these events and the brooding atmosphere in the apartment, the Bartells held a séance. They successfully contacted the spirits of a gray cat and a young woman who said she had lived at the house. Both seemed friendly, and the woman denied knowing anything about the source of any evil sensations the Bartells might be suffering. Of course, she was not necessarily telling the truth.

The séance did not alleviate the atmosphere; if anything, it deteriorated, eventually becoming so disturbing and suffocating that the Bartells decided to move away. They took an apartment on the Upper East Side. Here, they might have been free of ghosts, but their desperation for peace was ruined by the constant stream of people coming and going at all hours of the day and night in another apartment on their floor.

Loss of sleep for Jan Bartell was bad enough after her previous ordeal, but it especially took its toll on her husband, who managed a restaurant and often came home late. The Bartells were forced to move again.

The news that there was a vacant apartment at the building next door to number 16 West Tenth Street was received by the couple with mixed feelings. It was so close to the home that harbored such terrifying memories, but it was also in the house once owned by author Samuel Clemens—better known as Mark Twain. It seemed to them almost fateful that this opportunity arose, for not only had Jan and Fred always admired the property, but Fred was a Mark Twain buff and even the restaurant he managed was called the Mark Twain Riverboat.

Built in 1854, number 14 West Tenth Street was occupied by the author from 1900 to 1901. Before being converted into apartments, it was a single-family town house and that is how Twain and his family enjoyed the property. Although they had servants, his wife Olivia was in poor health and the large and imposing four-story house was too much for her to manage. This was the reason given for their move after just a year. Subsequent events suggest something far more sinister may have expedited their departure.

At first, life in the new apartment was perfectly normal for the relieved Bartells. But soon their nightmare returned. During their time at number 14, the Bartells heard of nine deaths in the apartments—residents and their pets dying in mysterious circumstances. This and other chilling events similar to those they had experienced next door provoked Jan to write a book, *Spindrift: Spray from a Psychic Sea*, about the paranormal happenings in the house. In this book, she wrote of twenty-two deaths that had questionable or mysterious aspects to them.

She told friends that the book, published in 1974, was a kind of catharsis. Jan described the deaths as a game of "nine little Indians" and included information gleaned from tenants about the house's history. One told her there were many stories of Mark Twain's ghost being seen back in the 1930s. Had the author returned to his old family home following his death in 1910?

There were also tales of sounds "like somebody walking around the walls wearing army boots" down in the basement. Even the real estate agent who managed the building had to admit the series of deaths could not be coincidence and declared with certainty that "This place is cursed!"

Jan herself, although only in her mid-forties, suffered constant ill health and, shortly after fleeing the house to New Rochelle, she died. The coroner's report listed a heart attack, but rumors abounded that she had committed suicide. Whichever is true, it is arguable that Jan Bartell's death was brought on by living in fear for so long.

The ghostly history of number 16 did not die with Jan Bartell. Others have come forward to report a plethora of unexplained phenomenon, including disembodied footsteps, the feeling of presence in a room when no one is there, loud crashing noises where nothing has fallen or broken, and the feeling of being followed. Most activity is said to occur in the section that was once the mansion's servants' quarters. It has been suggested that later renovations on the building confused the spirits and trapped them there.

In 1987, the house was once more at the center of attention, this time as the scene of one of the most horrendous crimes ever committed in that quiet, upscale part of Greenwich Village. Living on the third floor was Joel Steinberg, a lawyer in private practice who specialized in defending some notorious criminals. His clients included a great many drug dealers, and it was whispered that they frequently paid Steinberg in drugs.

Living with the lawyer was his common-law wife Hedda Nussbaum, a former children's book editor who had been so mentally and physically brutalized by Steinberg that she had literally become his slave. The couple did not live alone. The tragic scenario was completed by the illegal adoption by Steinberg of a little boy and girl. Steinberg acted under the pretext of arranging private adoptions for two unwed teenage mothers. Since

there were no formal procedures, the children slipped through the cracks of the system and were accepted as the Steinbergs' own by neighbors and teachers. No one, it seemed, recognized the telltale signs of abuse when little Lisa Steinberg attended school with bruises.

It was on the morning of November 2, 1987, that police and paramedics were called to Steinberg's apartment in the Mark Twain house. Lisa was lying unconscious on the floor and was rushed to St. Vincent's Hospital. She never regained consciousness and died a few days later. It soon became public knowledge that the little girl had been beaten to death by Joel Steinberg.

The court case provoked colorful stories from Steinberg's friends who insisted that, once a kind and honest man, he had changed beyond recognition after living in the apartment for fifteen years. Reference was made to Jan Bartell and her book. Supporters of Steinberg claimed number 16 was full of negative forces that pushed him to the breaking point. But to the court, it was an open-and-shut case. Steinberg was a child killer. He is still serving time in prison for Lisa's murder.

Whatever it is that haunts the two houses once occupied by Jan Bartell, it does not have a name. Unlike the other tales in this book, there is no person or persons in the building's history who are likely to be causing such an oppressive

atmosphere. It could be that the perpetrator of the evil within these walls was secretive during life or that some awful tragedy was enacted here that escaped detection. However, it could be that this is no haunting at all. The paranormal is not an exact science; it is full of contradictions and different opinions about even the simplest matters. It is entirely possible that the evil that haunts the old homes of the Bartells was never human but is altogether more primal and sinister. To hypothesize further, it seems odd that the one spirit who has been contacted here could not or would not give any information that might help toward understanding the haunting at West Tenth Street. Surely, something so powerful that it was palpable to the living would be obvious to a spirit? It did not occur to Jan Bartell, who took the spirit at its word, but tales of women accompanied by cats abound in literature. Could witchcraft be at work here? Such an idea is pure conjecture, but it might explain how dark forces could have been unleashed here, why it would have been secret, and why the woman and her cat cannot leave.

tHe SILeNt poet

tHe SILeNt poet

CHURCH of st. Luke's IN the fieLDs—187 HUDSON street

Through an upper window of the old rectory of St. Luke's can sometimes be seen a shadowy figure. It is unremarkable, you might think, to catch sight of someone through a window as they go about their business. But something about this man is arresting. He is not quite of this world, appearing gauzy and dressed in clothes that belong to a time long gone. The room was once the office of Clement Moore, author of the famous poem "The Night Before Christmas." Though the ghost has never spoken, it is widely believed to be the poet's specter, keeping a silent vigil over the church he once loved.

Clement Moore, son of Benjamin Moore, the Episcopal bishop of New York, served as a warden at St. Luke's while Manhattan was only just stirring itself and the new church actually did stand in the fields. He was a quiet, scholarly man who thought of his poetic hobby as rather frivolous. *"The Night Before Christmas,"* for example, was never meant for publication but to amuse the children around him.

Some ghosts keep their secrets better than others, and no one has managed to divine why Clement Moore would return to his old office so frequently after his demise. His life contained no great struggle or torment, and his death was of natural causes in ripe old age. To all who knew him, his life was long, successful, and spiritually satisfying, what each one of us hopes for and usually the least likely existence to produce a haunting. Yet his spirit has been seen many times, gazing from the window of what is now a thrift shop. Those who have puzzled over his mysterious reappearance can point to only two possible reasons for his return. The first of these is something that recurs fairly often in hauntings, and even within these pages: the disturbance of a person's remains can, it seems, reanimate their spirit. When Moore died, he was buried in a vault alongside St.

Luke's, but his body was moved, along with the church's other parishioners, late in the nineteenth century. The congregation had become divided on some church matter, and a group had broken away from the church and established a new St. Luke's far uptown in Washington Heights. Those who remained with the Hudson Street church chose to affiliate with Trinity Parish, New York City's oldest Episcopal church. The bodies buried in the old St. Luke's churchyard, including Moore's, were disinterred and reburied in Trinity's new uptown cemetery at Broadway and 155th Street. It is possible that Moore, whose family originally owned the land around St. Luke's and who helped develop it, is protesting at being moved away from the neighborhood that was his lifelong home.

The second reason is another that has brought more than one spirit back from the beyond. Like Peter Stuyvesant, Moore was something of a guardian figure in life, and as a deeply responsible and dutiful man, he could simply be keeping a paternal eye over his lands and fellow parishioners.

Though it is not possible to say with any certainty why the poet stares from his old window, there he remains as much a fixture of New York City as the church he loved. His haunting is an uncharacteristic gesture of defiance against all that he believed during life, but perhaps when death finally came for him his love for his neighbors, friends, and the familiar streets proved too strong to be resisted.

Above left: Very few people who walk by St. Luke's today or enjoy a rest in its gardens know of its connection with a man who changed America's celebration of Christmas. And they are even less aware that the man's ghost still watches over the church today. St. Luke's resident spirit is Clement Clarke Moore, author of "The Night Before Christmas."

Above: Some believe that Clement Clarke Moore acts as a guardian, watching over his church. Maybe this is why, although St. Luke's suffered a disastrous fire in 1981, which completely gutted the sanctuary, its walls survived and the church was able to rebuild within a couple of years.

THE HAUNTED INN

The elegant Victorian gentleman in a silk top hat has no name, or at least none that anyone can remember, but he has been a presence here at this quaint old inn throughout memory. His imposing figure is often glimpsed from the corner of an eye, making its way through the dining area, and unexplained occurrences are common here. Disconcertingly, the gentleman particularly enjoys playing with fire, and then there is the regular thudding of a heavy weight being dragged up the back stairs.

Hauntings are often frustrating. As we have seen previously, the reasons for a ghost to appear can be opaque: often the spirits involved were of ordinary people who died long ago and few or no clues remain to who they may have been in life and why they have chosen to stay. Mediums and paranormal investigators can sometimes shed light on a ghost's motives, or simple everyday research into a building's past might turn up some previously hidden information, but all too often the spirit will be capricious and uncommunicative or written records will have been lost, if they even existed in the first place. No single event may have been reported that stands in people's memories as

the beginning of a haunting, yet too many people have seen the ghost and its activities or heard the mysterious sounds it makes for the stories to be dismissed.

Why the gentleman at the Waverly Inn frequents the place is unknown, and probably unknowable, though his presence here is routine. Over time many have proposed theories, but none seem to add up. The poet Robert Frost was once a frequent visitor here, and some argue that the ghost is his, troubled by his wartime experiences. But if so, Frost would be in disguise, for there is no other reason for him to be wearing Victorian garb. Others say the specter is that of Alexander Hamilton, who also has connections to the

area, but again the costume is from the wrong period. It is more likely that this ghost is of someone who was unremarkable in life but linked to the inn by some unusual event.

The ghost's traits are familiar to those who have experienced such things before: cold spots that cause the hair to prickle, noises that cannot be accounted for—even in a creaky old building that has passed it 150th birthday—the turning on and off of lights, objects that move, and fleeting manifestations that lead the witness to question whether what they thought they saw could possibly be real. However, unlike other spirits, the gentleman also plays with fire, literally: either putting them out or causing the fire in the grate to burst into a fresh explosion of flame.

When the building caught ablaze in 1996 and no reason could be found, suspicion rested on the gentleman. It seemed particularly odd that the room with which he is most associated, the dining room (which was once the smoking room), was completely untouched by the inferno, while the rest of the premises were not so lucky. Could it be that some event took place here that might cause the gentleman to want to burn the place down? It is the sound of a weight being dragged upstairs that particularly scares the staff. With such spooky goings-on it is obvious that their imaginations will turn to morbid explanations, but nevertheless, to those who hear it, the sound does put them immediately in mind of a body being dragged by rough hands to an upstairs room.

DyLaN thomas's favorite HauNt

WHite HORSe taverN—567 HUDSON Street

In Dylan Thomas genius and alcohol combined to produce a difficult, contrary man, one capable of producing great art even while struggling with alcoholism. His final drinking binge took place at the White Horse Tavern. After sinking nineteen whiskies, he staggered out and was admitted to a hospital a few hours later. His liver may have failed him, but that does not prevent the great poet from returning to his favorite haunt, to sit at the table he prefers and turn it, as always, to the correct angle to write at. Where once the poet was the center of attention, now his spirit sits alone and brooding in the dark, too stubborn to leave the place where he brought about his own death.

Thomas's personality in life once led Truman Capote to describe him as an "overgrown baby who'll destroy every last thing he can get his hands on, including himself." It was a prescient criticism, for soon after the author of *Under Milk Wood* was dead, self-poisoned with alcohol. He was an arrogant man in life, and it may be that having died while so confused by the massive amounts of liquor he had imbibed that the poet's spirit does not accept death. It might simply be that Thomas finds the convivial, atmospheric bar preferable to whatever else

the afterlife holds. Whatever the reason for his continued patronage, Dylan Thomas still holds court at the White Horse Tavern. The fact is so ingrained in New York legend that another poet, Stephen Roxborough, even wrote a poem in 2003 in which the two writers, one alive and the other dead, go on a drinking spree around the city.

The Welsh poet arrived on American shores in 1950 to give a series of lectures, and it wasn't long before he was introduced to the White Horse by fellow Celt and poet, the Scottish Ruthven Todd. The bar is a fine old

Opposite: Welsh poet Dylan Thomas was a hard drinker for most of his adult life, but there was no question as to which was his favorite haunt in Manhattan—the White Horse Tavern on Hudson Street in Greenwich Village. This rare picture of Thomas, showing him sharing a whiskey with the proprietor, was taken only months before his untimely death after collapsing at this very same bar at the end of a drinking spree.

wood-framed building, built back in 1880, and in those days it had turned from being the hangout of longshoremen to a center of literary activity, attracting the likes of novelists Norman Mailer, James Baldwin, Anaïs Nin, and Jack Kerouac. In these heady intellectual surroundings, Thomas gave full rein to his habit of drinking prodigiously, quaffing oceans of ale and spirits in the tavern's back room and establishing the place as his New York headquarters. Indeed, his regular presence became so well known that tourists would throng the bar to watch the curly headed Welshman drink himself into oblivion. It must have seemed strange that such an uncontrollable drunk could reach inside himself and find such beauty of expression.

Left: The White Horse, founded in 1880, is the oldest bar in the West Village. It started in the corner building in a former livery stable built in 1817 and grew until it took over two other nineteenth-century structures.

However, there were quieter moments at the White Horse also. During the day Thomas would be found at his favorite table by the window in the back room. Aside from the occasional visit to the bar to refresh his glass, he would sit there and compose his poetry. When he did so it was his habit to adjust the furniture to the most comfortable position—turning the little square table around so that one of its points formed the top of his writing space.

It was a November evening in 1953 that Thomas's excesses finally caught up with him. Despite his best intentions to stay sober to prepare for an upcoming lecture tour, Thomas found it hard to break his old habits once inside the warm and comfortable place he knew so well. He ordered a cheeseburger and French fries and an apple pie. Then he ordered a whiskey. And then another. When Thomas finally staggered out of the White Horse Tavern, he had downed nineteen shots—a new record even for such a prodigious drinker. He barely made it back to the Chelsea Hotel before collapsing.

Thomas was taken to nearby St. Vincent's Hospital suffering from inebriation and severe liver failure. After being in a virtual coma for several days, the poet who had written the words "Do not go gentle into that good night" went into the night for the last time.

To lose such a brilliant mind at the age of only thirty-nine was a great loss to literature,

but anyone with the patience to wait through the empty nights in the back room of the White Horse Tavern might be rewarded by a visit from a short, plump, curly haired figure with a gift for words. At the end of each night, all of the tables in the room that is now named for Thomas are lined up, ready for the next day's business. At least once or twice a month when staff return the next morning, there is always one that has been adjusted, turned so that the point would provide the top of a writing space. It is the same table by the window at which Dylan Thomas habitually sat.

Perhaps what brings him back is the memory of the whiskey he can no longer drink, or the sounds of drunken literary arguments long past, or maybe he comes simply to recall the thrill of knowing that the people who are standing eight deep at the bar are there only to catch a glimpse of him. For whatever reason the poet makes his regular pilgrimage, in death it seems that he is no longer the hell-raising drunk. When the staff return the next day there is no trace of him but the telltale repositioning of his table. Maybe he now simply sits and composes in his favorite haunt. Perhaps as he does so he ponders on his own words: "Bring out the tall tales now that we told by the fire as the gaslight bubbled like a diver. Ghosts whooed like owls in the long nights when I dared not look over my shoulder . . ."

aLexaNDeR HamiLtoN stiLL waLks

JaNe stReet, BetweeN HUDSON aND WaSHINGtON stReets

While his old enemy and killer tips glasses and pushes people down the stairs

of the old carriage house turned restaurant that once formed part of his prop-

erty, Alexander Hamilton's shade has been seen by many around Jane Street.

It was to a house in this area that his dying body was brought after the fateful

duel with Aaron Burr. Two hundred years later, he still walks the streets and

into houses, never at rest. And, like his nemesis, Hamilton's presence is strong

enough that his ghost can—and often does—interfere with the physical world.

While Aaron Burr may have been the victim of numerous tragedies, including the murder of his beloved daughter, his archenemy and rival has only one reason to stalk Jane Street. A brilliant man at the height of a remarkable career, his was a senseless death at the hands of someone whom in life he had despised and thwarted at every opportunity. If there is consciousness after death, Hamilton would have been incensed to see Burr elude justice for his murder. Perhaps unable to resolve his terrible anger, he returns, agitated, night after night to vent his spiritual energy, while at the same time indulging his well-known curiosity—flicking light switches, turning on radios, and meddling with other contraptions that would have been alien to his world. Perhaps so long after the deaths of all the principals in this story, there can never be a resolution and his ghost is doomed to walk Jane Street forever.

We have already briefly encountered the famous duel between Burr and Hamilton from the former's point of view. It was an event that has had reverberations down through the centuries that have followed, including chaining at least one man's soul to the physical world. As such it deserves fuller account than it was given in Burr's tale, so let us return to New York in 1804 and look at the events again through the eyes of the man

Opposite: A portrait of Alexander Hamilton. The story of Hamilton's tragic death is well known to every student of American history. His feud with Aaron Burr stretched all the way back to the American Revolution, when both men served in the Continental Army under General George Washington's command. In death it seems that both are doomed to remain in the mortal world, perhaps until their vendetta is resolved.

Today at 62 Jane Street stands an apartment house built in the 1880s that carries a plaque marking it as the site where Alexander Hamilton died. But this is just a guess, for the truth is that we really don't know where William Bayard's farmhouse was located. It must, however, have been within the blocks between Washington Street and Hudson Street, because in 1804 the shore of the Hudson River was at today's Washington Street (subsequent landfill having greatly expanded Manhattan's waterfront).

Wherever the house stood, his connection with it does not seem to prevent Hamilton's spirit from moving around the neighborhood, for he is often seen in the street or in different houses. Unlike Burr, though, his ghost appears to hold only benevolence to the people that populate his modern haunt. On one occasion he saved a Jane Street resident from harm. She had just had some new shelves installed in her kitchen but didn't realize that the carpenter had neglected to brace them properly. As soon as the shelves were up, she loaded them with heavy pots and pans, putting a strain on their weak supports. Suddenly the ghost of Hamilton appeared, frightening the woman so badly that she jumped away from the shelves—just before they tumbled to the ground. Had Hamilton not appeared, she might have been hit by falling objects and perhaps seriously injured.

There is something in the events that occurred around these two men that has spawned a disproportionate amount of ghost stories. Already we have met Eliza Jumel, who is accused of murder by her dead husband, and there is at least one other ghost linked to the two men. As it directly touches another story in this book, it is worth noting that Hamilton and Burr's mutual animosity did not prevent them working together from time to time and they once formed part of the highly effective defense team in the infamous trial of Levi Weeks, the young man indicted for the murder of Guliana Sands, who is now said to haunt a bistro in Spring Street (see page 134).

Perhaps the strength of loathing between these two such passionate people is too great to have dissipated, and these other ghosts as well as their own are simply tiny echoes of momentous events in their lives somehow recorded or sustained by the monumental bitterness of their resentment. Such things have been reported, and it would certainly provide an explanation if Alexander Hamilton behaved like a "recording ghost." However, Hamilton, like Burr, seems capable of interacting with the world and with people, which signals a consciousness rather than a simple playing out of old events. It seems that death was simply not enough to overcome the two men's rage and, at least on Hamilton's part, his hatred keeps him bound to the city where he lost his life to a bullet.

Ghosts of the ship of doom

The Riverview Hotel was once the American Seaman's Friend Society, built in 1907 to offer lodgings to the captains and first officers of the luxury liners of the period. It was to here that the grief-stricken, frightened survivors of the *Titanic* wreck were brought after the ship that saved them—the *Carpathia*—berthed in New York. The building harbors those memories yet. Moans of despair, mysterious wisps, multiple cold spots, and elevators that arrive unsummoned have prompted the legend that when the survivors arrived, they brought with them the terrified, suffering souls of friends and loved ones who perished with the ship.

When the *Titanic* slipped beneath the waves on the cold night of April 15, 1912, she took with her over fifteen hundred passengers who may have been saved but for the lack of lifeboats. Those lucky enough to find a place in one later spoke of watching the great ship as she wallowed lower in the water, the lights on board going out suddenly, the band finally silenced, and the screams of 1,512 passengers and crew mingling as the *Titanic* began her final descent into the Atlantic. The screams did not last long; soon all was eerie silence save the sobs of those floating in the vast Atlantic on their few pathetic craft. Those poor people still on the ship would have died quickly in the icy waters, being sucked into the immense pressures of the deep by the passage of the massive ship. As their souls departed their frozen bodies, where would they go, in their bewildered pain and sorrow, except with the few who survived?

It was a long night for those in the lifeboats until the heroic crew of the *Carpathia* arrived. She was the first to respond to the *Titanic*'s distress signals, but still many hours too late to do anything but take aboard the survivors. Her crew dutifully did so and treated these poor, haunted people with tender compassion as they completed their Atlantic voyage.

When *Carpathia* arrived at New York Dock (now known as Pier 54), the terrorized survivors were taken to the American Seaman's Friend Society. Here they could rest, eat, and sleep away from the eyes of the world for a night or two and begin the daunting task of picking up their broken lives. But it seems that even from the beginning those who came to the society brought more with them than they realized. Never before had the building been troubled by any kind of paranormal activity; it was only five years old, after all. But since the arrival of the *Carpathia*'s unusual complement, the place has abounded with the type of phenomena that are so familiar from "classic" hauntings.

When the building changed use and the old ballroom became a theater, the cast began to tell of peculiar events they had seen, heard, or felt between and during performances, and the staff of what is now the Riverview Hotel tell of the same experiences. Disembodied moans and the sobs of loss can be heard in the corridors, and the occasional indistinct figure is seen wandering aimlessly as if not sure of its whereabouts, a feeling of numbing coldness arrives from nowhere and departs as rapidly. Those who have spoken about the

occurrences there speak of an impression that there are many souls, each bonded in some tragedy. It would appear that those who died aboard the *Titanic* were cast adrift on the sea like their luckier fellows, and, with nothing but the ocean to cling to, they too were picked up by the intrepid *Carpathia*.

Above: Although the Riverview is now a busy budget hotel, some people maintain that it is still visited by passengers of the *Titanic*—those who never made it to dry land.

the shade of the ziegfeld follies

At the beautifully restored New Amsterdam Theater, Olive Thomas—"The Most Beautiful Girl in the World"—still takes center stage as she did when this was the home of the glamorous Ziegfeld Follies. In her hand she clutches the small blue bottle that was the last thing she saw in life. Is Olive trying to tell us something of her death from across the years? Or can her shadow simply not tear herself away from the scene of those lavish productions, when she was the star and had the world at her feet? Perhaps even just the memory of the spotlight is preferable to the dark beyond death.

Olive's story takes place in the New York of the Roaring Twenties, the jazz age, a dazzling, glittering New York of cocktails and shows, where talent could be found on every street corner. It was a place in which Olive Thomas was vibrantly alive, the center of attention. When she made her entrance it was invariably to the rapturous applause of an endless sea of audiences. But like so many ghost tales, hers contains an element of mystery; the events surrounding her death have never been fully explained. Why, we could ask, is Olive's melancholy figure still seen so often on the stage of the same theater that witnessed her greatest triumphs? And why did she leave life just as it seemed that all her dreams of stardom were coming true?

In a town that boasted a bewildering array of theaters, none was more famous or more spectacular that the New Amsterdam. It was here that Florenz Ziegfeld staged his "Follies," incredible revues of singing, dancing, costume, and light at the center of which was always the female form. Ziegfeld chose his girls for talent as well as beauty, but Olive Thomas was one of the most lovely of an extremely glamorous group. Her looks and talent were considered on a par with silent film stars

Right: A typical act from the New Amsterdam Theatre: the Cameron Sisters, who were featured in the "Ziegfeld Nine O'Clock Review" of 1916. No productions were more exciting, lavish, or daring than the famous Ziegfeld Follies. Producer Florenz Ziegfeld devoted his life to providing spectacular entertainment and "glorifying the American girl." To be one of Ziegfeld's chosen chorus girls became the dream of many young women all over America.

of that time such as Mary Pickford, Clara Bow, and Louise Brooks. Ziegfeld, for one, was unable to resist her, and he was never a man to let his marriage interfere with womanizing. The two had a short affair, which ended like so many others when his eyes rested on another beauty, but Olive was a sophisticated girl of her time, and the relationship cooled into a friendship without any sign of rancor. Indeed, it would be Ziegfeld who paid for her funeral. Besides, Olive was in demand elsewhere and was soon traveling to Hollywood to star in film after film. Though she would eventually make over two hundred movies, only one of her films is still in existence. It is desperately sad that a woman with so much talent and beauty, who was on the verge of becoming one of Hollywood's greatest leading ladies when she died, should now be almost completely forgotten by all but a few film historians and, of course, those who have witnessed her ghost on the stage of the New Amsterdam.

It was in Hollywood that Olive met and married movie actor Jack Pickford, younger brother of the actress Mary Pickford. Although not as famous as his sister, Jack enjoyed a successful career playing all-American college types. But beneath his happy-go-lucky public persona, there was a dark side to his character. There were rumors of gambling, drinking, and drugs. The marriage was stormy.

Jack and Olive separated, only to reconcile a few months later. To celebrate, they took a second honeymoon to Paris. One night in their suite at the Ritz Hotel, Olive got up and went into the bathroom without turning on the light, to keep from disturbing Jack. When he awoke a few hours later, Jack found Olive lying dead on the bathroom floor with a small cobalt blue bottle by her side. The bottle contained bichloride of mercury, a lethal poison when taken in sufficient quantity.

Jack said that he was sure Olive's death was accidental and thought she had reached for a bottle of antacid, picking up the wrong bottle in the dark. However, the question was: what was the bichloride of mercury doing in the medicine cabinet? In those days, its only medicinal use was as a treatment for syphilis. Did Jack have the disease? Had he infected Olive? Had Olive taken the drug on purpose because of problems with their marriage? Or did Jack, tired of the constant arguments, decide to put and end to them in the quickest way possible? No evidence has ever come to light of Jack Pickford murdering his wife, and it would be a strange choice of poison if he had, but if we are to believe the reports of Olive's ghost carrying a small blue bottle, it would seem that it has some great meaning to her spirit.

Whatever the answer, Jack seemed inconsolable. On the ocean liner bringing Olive's body back to New York, he attempted

to jump overboard and had to be physically restrained by the other passengers. Ziegfeld paid for Olive's lavish funeral and her burial at the beautiful and fashionable Woodlawn Cemetery in the Bronx, but he wouldn't attend the service—or anyone else's funeral for that matter. Perhaps he was superstitious; perhaps he preferred to remember Olive as she was in life.

The Follies, meanwhile, carried on as usual, but perhaps Olive took exception to others reveling in the stardom snatched away from her, for strange events soon began occurring around the New Amsterdam. Objects moved mysteriously backstage. Theater workers glimpsed fleeting shadows in the wings. The Follies had their last season at the New Amsterdam in 1931, although this did not keep Olive's ghost from taking the stage from time to time; even the conversion of the theater to a movie house in the 1940s failed to end her appearances.

A young electrician described seeing a beautiful girl on stage early one morning before the theater opened. As he told his story to one of the veteran stagehands, the older man's face turned white—for he, too, had seen the ghost years before. She always appeared wearing a white dress, with a gold sash elegantly draped across the bodice and over one shoulder. A few days later, the two men found some Follies memorabilia in one of the offices above the theater's entrance. It was a tradition every year at the opening of a new Follies season to take a "class picture" of all the cast members. Naturally, Olive Thomas was there in many of the lineups, smiling as sweetly as ever. It was as if she was smiling at the men who now gazed at her image—for it was her ghost, of course, who had appeared before them.

The New Amsterdam fell into a poor state of repair and closed down as a movie house. Conservationists, however, recognized its rich history as home to the Follies and, as New York's most notable example of an Art Nouveau–style theater, certainly deserved preservation. The Forty-second Street Redevelopment Company launched plans to save it and began preliminary repairs—during which period Olive's ghost was frequently seen by the workmen.

The full restoration of the New Amsterdam became a reality when it was acquired by the Walt Disney Company as their home theater in New York for live stage events. The theater has been authentically and beautifully restored, using historic photos from the Follies period, so that it looks just as it did when Olive performed there. Elaborate plaster decoration, in the form of flowers and greenery, again covers almost every surface; the original colors of dark green, rose, and brown have been replicated, and even the theater's side boxes, removed when it became a movie house, have been meticulously reconstructed. Perhaps the restoration of her theater has bound Olive's spirit even closer to the New Amsterdam, for her ghost gives no indication of leaving.

Olive's death was among the more notorious of the Hollywood scandals of the time, rivaling that of the Fatty Arbuckle sexual assault case. Whether it was murder, suicide, or simply an accident is now a secret that will never be told. Certainly theatrical ghosts are not unusual: the applause that was such a lure in life draws a number of notable performers back from beyond death, even if, like Olive, they can only look out on an empty house. Olive's ghost perhaps feels more than most the fleeting quality of fame. Her movies are gone, and she was never allowed the opportunity to fully become the legend she could have been. Perhaps that is why she clutches still the little blue bottle that killed her. However it happened, the bottle is to blame for her fading memory where her name should have been unforgettable.

Opposite: Olive Thomas was propelled to stardom when she won a competition to find the most beautiful girl in New York. After a brief spell as a Ziegfeld girl she went on to movie stardom at seventeen. She made her movie debut in 1916, completed four movies in 1917, three in 1918, and six in 1919. She was just twenty-one when she died.

the ghost of the ROUND table

algonquin hotel—59 west forty-fourth street

Strange, that from lovely dreamings of the dead

I shall come back to you, who hurt me most.

You may not feel my hand upon your head,

I'll be so new and inexpert a ghost.

Perhaps you will not know that I am near—

And that will break my ghostly heart, my dear.

—Dorothy Parker, from "*I Shall Come Back*"

Loss, suicide, and emotional pain reverberate through the life of America's foremost woman of letters. Hers was a difficult life riven by contradiction: she was the seemingly careless socialite, always ready to burst an ego with her needle-sharp, casual wit, but inwardly seething with morbid thoughts and driven by her own darkness into the arms of often unsuitable men. She thought and wrote about death often, so perhaps it is not significant that she wrote the words above, but it is nonetheless strange that she could have predicted her own return from the dead. A woman educated in many different kinds of wisdom, perhaps she knew that it is often the most tortured souls who find it difficult to find rest in the afterlife. If so, she would have recognized in herself one who was destined to linger in death, a wraith trapped in the world of the living by her own pain. Perhaps she even found amusing irony in the fact that those who most need it cannot find the peace that was missing in life.

Dorothy Parker was a central figure of New York's literary set in the young twentieth century and, as a young writer establishing a dazzling reputation, a founding figure of the most prestigious luncheon club in the city. Known as the "Round Table" after their preferred table in the Rose Room of the Algonquin Hotel (and of course with a

Opposite: Of all the writers who sat at the Round Table, Dorothy Parker is perhaps the one most associated with the Algonquin. Her acerbic and witty words were often quoted in newspapers and magazines, and she was one of the first to be offered free lodging by the proprietor Frank Case when he realized the worth of having such colorful clientele. Today, her spirit is said to reside still at the hotel.

witty nod to Arthurian legend), the loose group of brilliant acquaintances included Robert Benchley, Alexander Woollcott, Zelda and F. Scott Fitzgerald, Heywood Broun, and George S. Kaufman, all the greatly admired writers and journalists of the day. So celebrated did the group become that soon stars like Harpo Marx and Douglas Fairbanks heard of the gatherings and started to drop by, too. The inner world of Dorothy Parker is difficult to judge with any accuracy, but those who knew her said that the afternoons at the Algonquin were the happiest times of her life.

Outside of the group and their scintillating conversation, life was quite different. Submitting to her own wild recklessness and abandoned sexuality, Dorothy engaged in many affairs, quite often with men who were very much her intellectual inferior. Some of these relationships proved so traumatic that Dorothy was twice driven to attempt suicide.

Above: Fritz Foord, Wolcott Gibbs, Frank Case, Dorothy Parker (seated left to right), Alan Campbell, St. Clair McKelway, Russell Maloney, and James Thurber (standing left to right) at an Algonquin cocktail party to celebrate the success of Case's book *Tales of a Wayward Inn,* in November 1938.

These suicide attempts were acknowledged in Parker's black humor poem, "*Resume*," when she said that having failed with razors, guns, and gas, "one might as well live."

In work, too, she was undisciplined. Finding escape from her demons in a full social calendar, she lost a lucrative job at *Vanity Fair*, though she was lucky enough to win other work, including at the *Saturday Evening Post* and the *New Yorker* (founded by her friend Harold Ross, another Round Tabler).

In 1927, when Hollywood became desperate for scriptwriters, Dorothy and some of her friends made the trek to Los Angeles, where she eventually married, divorced, and then remarried a young actor-writer named Alan Campbell. The two worked together on several successful screen projects, including *A Star Is Born*, before Alan died at their country estate in Bucks County, Pennsylvania.

When Dorothy moved back to New York in 1963, she did not return to the Algonquin.

It was no longer the place she had known, and most of her fellows from the Round Table were now dead. Instead, Dorothy made her home at a residential hotel, the Volney on East Seventy-fourth Street, with only her dogs for company. She died alone there on June 6, 1967.

But death did not signal the end for Dorothy. As predicted in those brittle, wistful lines written so long before, she returned. Not to haunt those who had hurt her most, but to the place that she had most loved in life and where she had perhaps felt most at home surrounded by her intellectual equals. It was certainly not long before staff and guests began to notice objects moving from where they had been put and dressing tables rearranging themselves. It would be like Dorothy to indulge in such clichéd behavior as a ghost. She would find humor in playing up to the expectations of a poltergeist. And she would have loved the hotel's famous "$10,000 martini." When ordering the drink, guests make an appointment with a jeweler and the drink is poured over the gemstone of their choice. Even Dorothy would have been impressed to have been bought one.

Many guests over the years have sworn they have seen the ghosts of the Round Table. Because of this, the hotel staff perform their own unique "exorcism" every New Year's Eve. At midnight, the kitchen crew enters the hotel lobby banging pots and pans to frighten off the spirits. Considering the reputation of the ghosts in question, many believe they are heartily entertained rather than alarmed by the noise.

One woman who was taking photographs at the famous hotel found that her pictures all came out with ghostly streaks. She refused to accept renowned "ghost cynic" James Randi's explanation that light was simply getting into her camera. This phenomenon has been noted many times by ghost hunters, and is generally accepted by them to show spirit energy.

But there are darker, more alarming tales than the mere shuffling around of cosmetics and streaky photographs. A singer, Susannah McCorkle, committed suicide when her contract to perform at the hotel's Oak Room was not renewed. Friends and family were mystified as to why such an intelligent woman—she spoke five languages, worked as an interpreter, and was also a prizewinning short-story writer—should react so violently to what most would consider a simple setback in her career. Susannah was only fifty-five when she jumped to her death from her Manhattan apartment, and, although her former husband and business manager, Dan Dinicola, said the singer had suffered from depression, one wonders if some curse was to blame. Some observers of the case could not help but recall how Dorothy Parker suffered from a similar dark malaise and how she had tried to take her own life. Perhaps McCorkle, another writer, was

somehow more in tune with the spirit of the dead woman who walks the corridors of the hotel.

And then there are the sightings. If guests and staff of the Algonquin are to be believed, then Dorothy is not alone at the hotel. Other figures from the Round Table have been spotted here too. Of course, with such a glittering history, it is likely that the hotel would be proud of their ghosts. The patronage of such famous guests was wonderful for business when they were alive, and it surely doesn't hurt to have them check in for eternity. With this in mind, it is easy to be cynical about the supposed ghosts at the Algonquin, but nevertheless there are one or two reports that are compelling in their accurate description of the Round Tablers. And it is easy to imagine such a troubled soul as Dorothy Parker's lingering in a place where she was once happy, perhaps predestined to resolve her own dark thoughts before she is able to find peace and the "lovely dreamings of the dead."

tHe BISHOP of BROaDway

tHe BISHOP of BROaDway

BeLasco tHeatRe—111 west foRty-fouRtH stReet

New York is prodigiously blessed with specters and shades from the dramatic world. As a city it has always had more than its fair share of theaters, but perhaps there is more to it than that—Europe, too, has an unusual number of famously haunted stages. Is there something in the creation of illusion night after night, the trapdoors and effects, and the paint and emotion, that predisposes those involved to return from the grave? Perhaps unlike the rest of us mortals, those who devote themselves to making the unreal seem real are more adept at drawing the curtain that separates life and death. Perhaps it becomes even less difficult when one's entire life has been devoted to the stage, as David Belasco's was.

As we have seen elsewhere in this book, sometimes a person becomes so associated with a building or locale that they cannot bear to be parted from it even when life is over. Despite their very different lives, David Belasco has much in common with Gertrude Tredwell. Like her, his life was completely bound up within four walls. In his case it was the running of the theater he named after himself that consumed his every waking hour. He even slept here in a special apartment served by a private elevator, from which he could step out into his domain. Although its cables were cut many years ago, the elevator can still be heard making its rumbling journey from the penthouse. Now as always, Belasco steps out, takes a seat in his box, and casts his critical eye across the action on stage.

An imposing figure smartly dressed and with a distinguished head of steel-gray hair, David Belasco was a restrained eccentric in life. The first thing that anyone noticed about him was that he appeared to wear a clerical

Opposite: The name David Belasco is not well known today, except to students of American theater history. But in the 1920s and 1930s, this writer, producer, and director was a major force on Broadway. He reached the pinnacle of his fame and influence when he built his own theater in 1907, immodestly naming it after himself. He so loved his creation that he not only worked there, he sometimes lived there, too.

Left: Belasco, with his imposing and dignified appearance highlighted by a full head of steel-gray hair, affected a curious manner of dress. In his day, men wore high starched collars, which were frequently detachable from their shirts. For some reason no one ever discovered, Belasco would turn his collar around, like a priest's collar.

collar around his neck. It was this, as well as his undoubted power, that inspired the nickname "the Bishop of Broadway." No one ever dared ask why he wore his starched collar back to front, but it is thought that he was paying silent tribute to the priests who taught him as a young Jewish boy at a Catholic school in his native San Francisco.

How his ghost has come to haunt the theater is less of a mystery. Very simply, no one can imagine anything beyond death that would be able to hold his attention the way

his theater could. It was not a building to him, but an extension of himself, and he ran it accordingly, with the same restrained eccentricity and love of perfection. Veteran cast members remember how he would push his actors to give their best, even if it involved some trickery. If a scene wasn't going well and he felt there was a problem with a particular cast member, Belasco would pretend to become highly irate, so angry that he would throw down his pocket watch and jump up and down on it until the timepiece lay in pieces on the stage. Then he would turn to the offending actor and say: "Look what you made me do, and my mother gave me that watch." Those who had worked with him before would turn away smiling; they well knew that he kept a whole drawer full of dollar pocket watches up in the apartment, but the trick worked—at least once per actor.

After late-night rehearsals, Belasco would take his private elevator up to the idiosyncratic home he had built into the very plans of the building, in order that he could stay here night after night in complete comfort. It consisted of an office, a reception room, and a bedroom, with luxurious paneling and green brocade wall coverings. Belasco could come and go without being seen by actors or audience members, a feature that he is said to have exploited to the full when entertaining many of his female leads. Another attribute was a peephole, through which he could watch a performance or rehearsal in progress on the stage below and suggest ways of improving it later.

His perfectionism was driven by great passion to be the best. And to Belasco the best meant that the plays he put on had the appearance of reality. If a play was set in the country, he insisted that the audience would "see the sun rising and hear the birds singing." One of Belasco's productions, *The Governor's Lady*, featured a scene in a New York City diner. Instead of ordering his set designer to replicate the setting, Belasco simply went out and purchased the interior of an entire Child's restaurant (a popular eating chain of the time) and even had actors cooking on stage.

Exhausted from a lifetime of producing an astounding 121 productions in New York alone, David Belasco finally retired in 1930. But without the glamour and excitement of the greasepaint and costumes, the elaborate sets, and the heartbreak and adrenaline of the theatrical world, his life became empty and meaningless. He died just a year later, and now he seems only too pleased to have returned to his beloved theater. Soon after his death, the cast was astonished to hear a ghostly noise in the elevator shaft once more, and it is legend among New York's thespians that if one looks up from the stage on any opening night, Belasco's impressive figure can be seen looking down on their work.

Though his voice is never heard, David Belasco's spirit permeates the atmosphere of the theater. His was a life devoted to bringing something that only existed as words on a page to vivid life. Over the years, the plays he put on explored the deepest themes of humanity, of death and love, passion and belief. Can we say with complete conviction that a man of Belasco's temperament and expertise in manipulating reality could not find some way back to his most beloved home?

Above: The influential Moscow Art Theatre director Constantin Stanislavsky (seen here wearing a black bow tie) pays a visit to David Belasco (in white collar) for his 1923 production of *The Merchant of Venice*.

a ghost in hell's kitchen

a ghost in hell's kitchen

428 west forty-fourth street

Demented with hunger, shame, and a two-centuries-old refusal to admit her own death, the wraith of Lucy Ryan plagued the nights of actress June Havoc for years. When professional psychics were called in, however, Lucy was finally able to spill her sad tale of starvation and rape in New York's Hell's Kitchen. Despite the best efforts of the mediums, though, Lucy will not leave and her noises still echo through the New York night.

It was shortly after moving into her four-story, redbrick house in the late 1950s that actress June Havoc began to hear the strange noises that interrupted her sleep. Night after night she lay awake listening to the mysterious bumps and bangs that no one else in the building heard and that no electrician or plumber could account for. Frustrated and tired, sometimes the darkest hours of the night would find her pacing the corridors and listening at doors trying to find the source of the sounds, but she was never able to—they seemed to flit from one location to another. Always close, but never in one place.

A determined lady who had first appeared on screen at the age of two, and who had made a career on stage and screen ever since, June was, however, not going to be evicted from her own house. And besides, it was a convenient base for her, near the television studio where she presented her weekday show. As the fifties turned into the sixties, she stuck it out night after night, suffering from constant headaches as well as fatigue but refusing to budge from her home. Finally, with obvious exhaustion, she began to talk about her problem on air. One viewer of June's TV show listened with interest as she spoke about her sleepless nights, her face showing obvious signs of tiredness. The viewer was a friend of paranormal investigator Hans Holzer, who suggested that the answer to June's trouble could be found in the realm of the supernatural. Holzer conducted several séances in June's haunted town house, one of which was filmed and

later broadcast on her show. During the televised séance, a small table was said to have levitated and knocked against a wall.

It was during another séance, however, that successful contact was made with June's resident ghost. Through British psychic Sybil Leek, the ghost told the gathering that her name was Lucy Ryan and that she had lived in 1792, right after the Revolutionary War. What Lucy said next was particularly eerie. She was very hungry— and she wasn't dead.

In subsequent séances, Lucy talked about her time in what she called "Hell's Kitchen," an area of open, undeveloped land bordering on the Hudson River. The area was uninhabited except for an occasional farmhouse. "Hungry Lucy," as she became known, said she had been with a group of citizens camped near a Continental Army division, both for protection and in the hope of buying food and supplies from the troops. In those days following the Revolution, before the Constitution was ratified and central government was in place, a general state of chaos prevailed, with each state making its own laws and printing its own money. The camped group knew that even if provisions were in short supply for civilians, the army would always be well fed and perhaps the troops would be willing to sell food to its camp followers.

But another, age-old reason held Lucy to the site. She had met and fallen in love with one of the soldiers, a young man named Albert who, when he was sent on maneuvers to New Jersey, had asked her to wait for him. True to her promise, Lucy waited. She is waiting still.

It was in another séance that Lucy's voice began to falter, and it became obvious that she was greatly distressed. Through the tears, she managed to blurt out that while waiting in that same field one night for her lover, she was set upon by drunken soldiers and raped. She could barely walk because of her injuries.

Exactly how Lucy died is unclear. For after her traumatic revelation through Sybil Leek, she did not "come through" again. There is speculation that she died after being raped—as much through shame as from the physical injuries. Or she might have died through one of the many illnesses that were rampant at that time.

The fate of the rest of the ragtag band of civilians is not known, but the best theory is that the majority of them died, either of famine or from some epidemic—not an uncommon thing in eighteenth-century New York, when the city was repeatedly ravaged by yellow fever and smallpox. Sybil Leek, while channeling Lucy's spirit, said that there had been a burial ground for the poor on the

site—yet city records disclose no burial grounds in this area. There may have been hasty, informal burials, however, especially if an epidemic had broken out.

Was Lucy buried on this site? June Havoc mentioned a strange patch in her backyard garden where, despite several efforts, nothing ever grew. Whatever the circumstances, the noises grew less intense after the séances. June, Sybil, and Holzer believed their summoning of the spirit had, in June's words, "made Lucy free to go wherever she wanted to go." But she added:

After three nights' blissful sleep, I was again awakened in the middle of the night. But instead of incessant banging and tapping there was this hideous screaming. And this time, it sounded like it was coming from within a box directly over me. The next day I called Holzer and told him be to be harsh with Lucy and tell her to go back. But she didn't. She returned the next night. It was some time later that Lucy seemed to finally accept her death and move on.

Eventually, June sold her house and retired to her Connecticut home. Today, the Hell's Kitchen neighborhood of Manhattan, notorious in the late nineteenth and early twentieth centuries for its crowded tenements and rough street gangs, has become a gentler, friendlier place, even adopting the name of

Left: June Havoc, photographed in 1954, just before the time when her Hell's Kitchen town house became troubled by the presence of Hungry Lucy. It has been suggested that the performer purchased a house that was built over the unmarked mass grave of New York's poor in the wake of the Revolution.

Clinton. However, the majority of New Yorkers still call the place Hell's Kitchen.

June Havoc's house still stands, a few doors east of the famous Actors Studio housed in a former Presbyterian church. And recently, local residents have told of strange knocks and bumps and bangs—not just confined to the second floor where June lived, but throughout the whole house. Perhaps Lucy Ryan is still active, demented with hunger, unrequited love, or the terrible burden of burning shame.

afterLife at the Dakota

west seventy-second street and central park west

Looming over Central Park, the Dakota is said to be home to a number of

spirits. Perhaps this is hardly surprising for such a grand old dame of New

York's skyline, and a dame with such a colorful history. The most famous, of

course, is the ghost of John Lennon, who met his violent death just outside.

Various witnesses say that he has appeared in the building where he lived with

his beloved wife, but his spirit is only one among the many that walk the

corridors. Lennon himself told of seeing a female wraith weeping in the

corridors. Edward Clark, who built the Dakota, keeps a watchful eye over his

investment, and residents speak of seeing visions of old-fashioned furniture

they don't own. More chillingly, a small golden-haired girl bounces her ball

along the hallways. Who she is no one knows, but despite her seeming

innocence, her appearance always portends a death in the building.

Some buildings garner a reputation that is based more on perception than reality. There are buildings across the world that are said to be haunted merely because they look as if they should be or because some tragic event once took place there. The Dakota not only looks spooky with its Gothic roofline reminiscent of some old European castle, but it was first in the public eye as the setting for *Rosemary's Baby*, the film adaptation of Ira Levin's supernatural thriller. In the 1968 film, Mia Farrow plays a woman who gives birth to a child of Satan, and the Dakota becomes the "Bramford" apartment block. As if this weren't enough to establish the building as haunted in the common perception, it later tragically became the site of one of the most senseless and arbitrary crimes imaginable

Opposite: This engraving from September 1884, just before the Dakota was officially opened, shows the interior courtyard entrance. The West Seventy-third Street gate was planned as a service entrance, but when delivery wagons found it hard to unload on the narrow street, that gate was locked and hardly opened except for funerals, when hearses arrived to take away the building's deceased. It soon became known as the "Undertaker's Gate."

when John Lennon was assassinated just outside its lobby. It is no wonder, then, that the Dakota is widely held to be somehow cursed, or at the very least a place that is no stranger to the supernatural.

It is always worth remembering that media coverage or the look of a property might alter expectations when investigating paranormal activity. Nevertheless, in the Dakota's case appearances are not deceiving. Not only have many witnesses—Yoko Ono among them—reported seeing the spirit of John Lennon here, but there appear to be other, older spirits, too. Some are benign, others less so. Apart from actual apparitions, there have been many instances of lights going on and off by themselves and the building's elevators stopping and starting erratically. Objects such as bags of trash have been seen to levitate, and during one rather frightening period, several fires started at various points in the building, seemingly without human involvement. One resident recounts looking up at his living room from

Left: Mia Farrow in a scene from
Rosemary's Baby. The Dakota was chosen
as the location for this movie because of
its imposing Gothic appearance.

outside the building and clearly seeing a gleaming crystal chandelier—a chandelier he didn't have. A few months later, when some repairs were being made to his apartment, the nub of a similar light fixture was discovered. Perhaps all of this could be rationally explained away, but when added to the eyewitness reports of ghostly manifestations, it seems that there is more going on in the Dakota Building than is immediately apparent in the physical world. It is possible that the following ghosts are responsible for all of these strange phenomena, but equally there may be still more dead walking the corridors of the Dakota than we currently know about.

Probably the Dakota's first ghost, and certainly the most frequently seen, is of a rather absurd figure: a small man wearing spectacles and an obvious toupee. However, his unprepossessing looks hide—or hid during his life—an astute business mind and one that knew how to gamble. Edward Clark did much to change the way that people lived in New York. His was the money that funded the building of the Dakota far uptown in a virtually undeveloped area (Central Park had not been entirely finished when it was built). As if this wasn't risky enough, the idea of luxury apartment living was barely socially acceptable in Gilded Age New York. Many of Clark's well-to-do potential tenants still thought that living under the same roof as other families was something the poor did in tenements. To overcome this prejudice, the first luxury apartment developers found it necessary to include many incentives and extras to attract interest. The Dakota offered massive suites of rooms, some as large as a modern suburban house, with living quarters for servants. It also boasted a restaurant exclusively for residents, laundry facilities in the basement, and every luxury imaginable at the time, including hydraulically driven elevators. In short, it was almost a self-contained world.

Perhaps his continued existence here is the curse of financial greed. Whatever death holds for Mr. Clark, it seems that he is too busy watching over his investment to leave. He does not appear anywhere in particular but roams the building, though he is more likely to appear if any modifications are being made. His can be a sudden and startling appearance, but his otherwise harmless apparition has been seen by so many that it is an accepted fact, a part of the Dakota's personality. One typical witness was an electrician repairing some of the building's old wiring. He turned from his work to find Clark standing over him, only to vanish again as rapidly as he had arrived. It was upon seeing a photo on one of the Dakota's walls that the workman was able to identify the ghost who had disturbed him.

Another of the Dakota's resident specters is less welcome. To those who do not know why her appearance should be so dreaded, the little girl in the old-style yellow taffeta dress bouncing a ball along the corridor might seem just a lonely and sad spirit. However, hers is a manifestation that

has been seen all too often at the apartment building—indeed, there are reports of her appearance going all the way back through the building's long history. Her spirit is a vanguard for death. When she is seen in the Dakota, someone in the building has been marked for the grave.

It is unknown if there is any relation between the two spirits, but in 1965, workers who were renovating apartment number 77 encountered the spectral form of a small boy who walked slowly down a hallway between two rooms. His is a ghost less often seen in the building, but on this occasion there were many witnesses who attested to his appearance.

But John Lennon's is the ghost that most famously haunts the Dakota. It was just outside the front lobby on December 8, 1980, that Mark David Chapman approached the former Beatle as he returned to his apartment clutching the tapes of that day's recording session. As Lennon got out of a limo, Chapman walked quickly up and asked quietly, "Mr. Lennon?" Before Lennon could answer, or even turn to face his assassin, Chapman raised a .38 and shot the star five times in the back. Lennon collapsed among his own blood and tapes. Within three minutes the police arrived to find Lennon dying and Chapman nonchalantly reading *The Catcher in the Rye*.

The death of one of the century's great icons made headlines around the world. But

Left: John Lennon, pictured here with his wife Yoko Ono, is the latest addition to the Dakota's family of phantoms. His ghost has been seen near the West Seventy-second Street gate where he was assassinated by Mark David Chapman in December of 1980, and crowds still gather every year in front of the gate to mark the anniversary of his death.

it is said that Lennon is still active. As you might expect for a star of his standing, crowds still gather each year on the day that he died to commemorate his life, and many have reported sighting his apparition in and outside the Dakota. In 1983, for example, Joey Harrow, a musician who lives near the Dakota Building, claimed he saw John's ghost in the West Seventy-second entrance. "He was surrounded by an eerie light," claimed Harrow. At the time of the sighting, Harrow was accompanied by writer Amanda

Moores, who confirmed that she had also seen the ghost. She said: "I wanted to go up and talk to him, but something in the way he looked at me said 'No.' "

In life Lennon was a pithy, realistic person with an earthy sense of humor, yet simultaneously intensely spiritual. He and Yoko Ono certainly had an interest in the occult, maybe fueled by the fact that they inherited a ghost when they purchased the large Dakota apartment of actor Robert Ryan, whose wife Jessie had died there.

Becoming curious, after several strange occurrences, the Lennons held a séance and confirmed that their resident spirit was indeed Ryan's late wife, who politely but firmly informed them that she had no intention of vacating "her" apartment.

Lennon was also aware of other presences around the Dakota and had a number of strange experiences of his own in the building. He once claimed to have spotted a flying saucer while looking out of the window (he even referred to it on his *Walls and Bridges* album) and also reported seeing a spectral figure walking down the corridors of the Dakota, which he referred to as "Crying Lady Ghost."

Despite these sightings, and Lennon's own belief in talking to the spirits of the dead, it is difficult not to be skeptical about some of the ghostly tales that surround him. It is perhaps inevitable that such a famous name will be used, even in death, by those who seek to make a name for themselves. One writer and medium has published a book complete with entire conversations with Lennon. In the publication *Idols: 20th Century Legends*, Deer Domnitz claimed to discuss with Lennon topics of a psychic and religious nature, astral travel, and life in the spirit world. There were also messages to Yoko Ono, their sons Sean and Julian, and Lennon's former fellow Beatles Paul McCartney, George Harrison, and Ringo Starr. For twenty-six months, the medium claimed

she spoke to Lennon and alleges that he disclosed to her that he was remaining close to Earth in order to save the planet from destruction and that he was working to further the cause of world peace and harmony. This is similar to messages about a "white brotherhood" of the spirit world, which Lennon reportedly discussed with other mediums.

Another psychic, Rosemary Brown from London, claimed that Lennon first arrived in her living room in 1984 and dictated over two dozen songs. Said Rosemary: "He is taller than I always imagined him in this life. I seem to see him as he looked at the height of the Beatles' early success. He looks to be in his late 20s or so, he is clean shaven, fresh-faced, doesn't wear glasses."

According to several "ghost-chasers," Lennon's spirit lingered on Earth for a short time after his death before a group of spirit guides helped him to adjust to the "other" world. (As we have seen so many times already in this book, a person who won't "let go" after death becomes a ghost who haunts the area of the tragedy.) The guides say they convinced him to join them in the spirit world, and various mediums began receiving messages from him.

However, if all of this sounds too odd to be true, then perhaps it should be remembered that John Lennon is the man who, in the name of peace, once spent a week with Yoko tied in a large bag in the lobby of a Viennese hotel.

With such a famous individual, it is difficult to separate truth from fiction, the honest sighting from the charlatan. Perhaps, though, we can trust the words of Yoko Ono Lennon. After all, she was closest to him and has the least to gain from fabricating ghost stories. Hers is a simple tale, told in a few words, and perhaps captures best the real spirit of John Lennon. Yoko relates that she saw John sitting in the apartment at his white piano. His ghost turned to her and said: "Don't be afraid, I am still with you."

So numerous are the hauntings at the Dakota that it is easy to dismiss them all out of hand. Nevertheless, amid all of the hysteria surrounding the Lennon myth and the resonance of the genuinely chilling *Rosemary's Baby*, there are many independently supported ghost sightings at the Dakota. If even half of them are true, it would seem that even for a large building with such a long history it has an ability to keep more than its fair share of souls within its walls. Could it be that there is something sinister beneath the surface at the Dakota?

Left: Yoko Ono sits at the famous white piano of her husband John Lennon in their apartment at the Dakota. It is at the piano that Yoko has reported seeing John's spirit.

a "SOUTHERN MANSION" IN manHattaN MORRIS-JUMEL MANSION—

65 JUMEL TERRACE AT 160TH STREET

Shunned by society in life and accused from beyond the grave of murder,

Eliza Bowen Jumel Burr is generally thought of by history as a scheming

adventuress. She ended her days here in a bed that once belonged to Napoléon

Bonaparte and surrounded by the trappings of wealth and luxury. Yet still she

has failed to find peace, and her shade is frequently seen, as spoiled and

irascible in death as she was in life. Is she too attached to her trinkets and

treasures to leave? Or is there some darker reason for her spirit to walk the

rooms and halls where once she scandalized New York?

The story of Eliza Bowen reads like a nineteenth-century novel. Her mother died giving birth to her in 1775 on the high seas during a passage from France. She was adopted by a woman from Rhode Island and grew up to abscond at age seventeen with a British officer. The young woman settled with her new husband in New York, where she soon scandalized society with her impulsive and arrogant behavior. Indeed, gossip portrayed "Betsy" as little better than a prostitute. Nevertheless, she was a great beauty and

soon acquired a coterie of influential male friends. Following the death of her first husband, she married a wealthy wine trader, Stephen Jumel, and the couple moved into the house that would remain Eliza's until her death, a hilltop mansion that had once served George Washington as headquarters during the Revolution. It was whispered that, longing to be seen as an "honest woman," she tricked Jumel into marrying her by feigning a fatal illness, from which she made a miraculous recovery after the "deathbed" wedding ceremony.

Even then the mansion was said to be haunted, by spirits that have continued to make their presence felt down through the years. Two teachers have separately attested to seeing the figure of a Revolutionary soldier on the top floor. This area of the house is also haunted by a young servant girl, who is said to have committed suicide after an ill-fated affair.

Soon after their marriage, Stephen and Eliza moved on to France, where Eliza won the friendship of Napoléon and spent a large portion of her husband's fortune in a whirl of fashion and parties. However, she proved herself a woman of great resource: on returning to New York she turned her talents to recouping the money she had dissipated on her travels.

In 1832 Stephen Jumel died following a carriage accident. The house and all his great wealth went, of course, to Eliza. At the time no one remarked on his death, but more recently his spirit has been contacted at the mansion on two occasions by eminent mediums Hans Holzer and Ethel Myers. During both séances he asserted the same thing: while recovering from his serious injuries, his wife had cruelly removed his bandages, then watched him bleed slowly to death. Understandably, Jumel's spirit was furious at a murder that went not only unpunished, but rewarded. For now Eliza was probably the wealthiest woman in the city and, again, at liberty.

Always the schemer, she now set her sights on the one thing that had always eluded her—social acceptance. And where marriage had served her well before, she concurred that it would again, particularly if she married a former vice president, even if his reputation was as tarnished by scandal as her own.

Eliza had known Aaron Burr since her days of dazzling drawing rooms with her beauty. The two were married in July of 1833, in the parlor of the mansion. Since the impoverished Burr was aged seventy-seven and his bride was fifty-nine, it was not the impulsive act of starry-eyed innocents, but a compact between two cynics. The outlook for a compatible union between two such strong-willed, volatile people was bleak, and after two years of marriage—and many fights and recriminations, mainly about his use of her fortune—Burr left Eliza, and she sued him for divorce. It was granted on September 14, 1836, the very day that Burr died in rented rooms in Port Richmond, Staten Island.

Despite becoming a widow and a divorcée on the same day, Eliza refused to forgo the little recognition she had gained as the wife of a famous politician. She would lean out of her carriage window and yell: "Make way for the wife of the Vice President of the United States!" At last, surrounded by money and with a veneer of social acceptability, she settled into comfortable old age in her mansion. She died, aged ninety, among her treasures on bedroom furniture, upholstered in blue, which she claimed had been a gift from Emperor Napoléon I.

Over the ensuing years the lands around the mansion have been swallowed up by the growing city, but the house remains and with it the imperious ghost of Eliza Bowen Jumel Burr. Never one to adhere to convention, she has not gone into death meekly but appears frequently to the house's visitors (it is now a museum). There are many reports of her apparition, but perhaps her most famous appearance was back in 1964 when she was seen and heard by an entire class of children. Having looked dutifully around the house, they had been allowed to go and play on the lawn outside and had become boisterous and a little rowdy. Their noise was brought to an abrupt halt by the aggrieved voice of an old woman, who had appeared on a second floor balcony wearing period dress of flowing purple. At first the spectators thought that she must be an actress, such was her tone and haughty figure, so after she had gone back inside the mansion, they asked the museum staff if they could meet her again. The bewildered employees said that there was no such person on the premises and asked the children to describe her. Their description fit Eliza perfectly.

After such a long and eventful life, one might think that Eliza deserves to be at

peace, so what keeps her here? Perhaps she simply likes her role as the independent lady of the manor too much to leave, but it seems a coincidence that another person whose life was touched by Aaron Burr should continue to haunt New York. Could there be more to their doomed relationship than is generally known to the history books? We know that theirs had been a long acquaintance and that they married only a year after the demise of Stephen Jumel, who has insisted to psychics that he was killed by Eliza. We can only guess at the dark secrets of people so long dead, but could it

be that Eliza, growing bored of her husband and feeling that his restored fortunes rightfully belonged to her, entered a murder pact with Burr? This would explain why Burr's ghost has been sighted here as well as at the restaurant that was once his carriage house.

Neither specter is likely to explain. Perhaps the only person who might be able to shed more light on the circumstances of his own death is Stephen Jumel himself. Unfortunately, due to the intervention of Holzer and Myers, his ghost is the only one to have departed the mansion for good.

Above: The dining room of the house, which more resembles a Southern plantation mansion than a New York home, was built in 1765 by Roger Morris, a Tory who fled the city during the Revolution. Eliza Jumel Burr, the wife of Aaron Burr and former mistress of the mansion, is said to wander through the house in a purple dress, rapping on walls and windows.

tHe OtHeR HaUNteD IsLaND

tHe OtHeR HaUNteD IsLaND

OLD BeRMUDa INN——2512 ARtHeR KILL ROAD, StATeN IsLaND

Martha Mesereau's story is a recurring one throughout history. She fell deeply in love, married, made a beautiful home, and looked forward to filling it with children and happiness, only to have her peaceful existence blighted by war. Having starved herself to death upon hearing of her husband's passing, Martha Mesereau waits for him nearly a century and a half later, softly pacing through the house and keeping a light shining in the window to guide him home from some distant battlefield. Until then she waits alone with her sorrow, often seen by guests but with her head bowed in grief and loneliness.

Today's Staten Island is a reminder of how Manhattan must have looked before development took over every inch of the island. In places it is wild and untamed, with rolling hills and saltwater marshes near the shore. Here you could almost imagine yourself miles away from the strident dazzle of the big city, particularly if you sit beside the fire at the Old Bermuda Inn.

It was here in the days when Victoria ruled across the ocean that a pair of newlyweds, Mr. and Mrs. Mesereau, made their home. They were a young couple looking forward to a promising life in their handsome house atop a hill overlooking the harbor. Like their neighbors, they preferred the empty spaces and fresh air to the dirty and claustrophobic city over the river.

However, their rosy future was soon cut short by the harsh reality of the Civil War. Mr. Mesereau was drafted into the Union army and, like a good patriot, went off to battle. His wife, like so many others around the riven country, patiently waited at home for her beloved's return. She waited in vain. When the news eventually came that he had been killed in action, her reaction was extreme. She locked herself in one of the small upstairs bedrooms, refused to eat, and finally died of starvation.

Left: The ghost of Martha Mesereau has been known to cause fires to burst into fresh flame from time to time. How and why her own portrait came to catch fire remains unexplained, however. Could it be that she is so confirmed in her grief that the sight of herself in happier days just causes more pain?

HISTORIC OLD
BERMUDA INN
MAIN ENTRANCE
AND PARKING

But love, it seems, conquers even death. Martha has never left her home, though it has gone through numerous owners and many additions. Now it is a wonderfully inviting inn at its heart, though it remains recognizably the house that the Mesereaus moved into, right down to the portrait of Martha standing in front of the parlor's fireplace. Her lovelorn shade is most often seen in the very room where her likeness was taken, though she often wanders the main staircase too, going from room to room in restless grief.

There are many who tell stories of Martha's haunting; hers is a constant presence here, and over the years she has startled many with her appearances and the usual inexplicable bumps and bangs that are associated with a resident ghost. As her specter wanders the building, she touches people with the freezing spots so often noticed when the dead are present, but most perplexing is a door in one of the upstairs rooms that keeps opening by itself, even when latched. No one knows why this should be so, unless this room is one that she particularly links to her absent husband.

There have also been strange incidents in connection with the inn's six original fireplaces, and on several occasions fires have blazed up without human intervention. Fire also played a part in what is perhaps the strangest recent happening. Martha Mesereau's portrait hangs above a table in

Above: Although the inn has been enlarged with a modern wing, which serves as a catering hall for banquets, wedding receptions, and private parties, the original 1832 house lies at the heart of the complex.

the entrance hall. During renovations the picture inexplicably caught fire. The blaze was quickly extinguished, but the scorched portion of the canvas can be seen to this day.

The most persistent phenomenon at the inn, however, is a sole light that turns on by itself after all other lights have been turned off for the night. The light shines like a beacon in the dark—almost as if Martha is watching from her window for her husband's return and shining a light to guide him.

As you might expect, the inn has been visited by a number of paranormal research groups. Though it seems somehow wrong that investigators would intrude on Martha's grief, their efforts have been rewarded with success. One group recorded strange sounds

in the little bedroom where Martha pined away. They also photographed a glowing orb in that room, and another on the staircase.

All of us hope that in death we will be reunited with the ones we love, but for Martha this has not been the case. Perhaps her husband, like so many of his fellow soldiers, haunts a now empty field that once saw a bloody campaign. It might be that he too cannot face eternity without his beloved wife. If his spirit is tied to the place of his death, it could be that the two will wait for all eternity. But perhaps one day his wraith will make its weary way back to the home they made together all those decades ago and Martha will finally be able to leave the Old Bermuda Inn behind.

Above: A bird's-eye-view photograph of Staten Island taken in 1905. The island was appealing enough to draw many well-to-do citizens to build luxurious homes there during the Victorian period, and there are a number of beautiful old houses still remaining.

tHat was NO LaDy!

tHat was NO LaDy!

FORMER CUSTOM HOUSE—1 BOWLING GREEN

Where the U.S. Custom House now stands was once the site of Fort
Amsterdam. It was here that Edward Hyde, Lord Cornbury, New York's royally
appointed governor—a cousin of Queen Anne herself, no less—would walk
along the battlements. From this vantage point he could survey the colony he
was so keen to extort while the breeze rustled his skirts picturesquely and
lifted the feathers of his fine bonnet. Cornbury is still here, arrogantly flouncing
along the corridors of the Custom House in a city that despised him. In death,
as in life, he prefers to promenade dressed as a woman.

In a city noted for its colorful characters, there have been few New Yorkers as outrageous—or as hated—as this mendacious and eccentric British aristocrat. During his short term as governor of New York and New Jersey (1802–1808), he alienated virtually the entire population: taking bribes for promises left unfulfilled, embezzling funds allocated for the defense of the city, and purloining lands and money. Indeed, one of his contemporaries noted that Cornbury was "a spendthrift, a grafter, a bigoted oppressor and a drunken vain fool." To make matters worse, many recorded histories tell us that he was an open cross-dresser: a lifestyle unremarkable today and a surprisingly acceptable peccadillo in aristocratic European circles at the time, but to the sober early New Yorkers an inconceivable perversion. Perhaps if his memory was not so besmirched with corruption and oppression at worst he would have been a laughable figure, but he is often recalled as the most unpleasant governor in New York's long history.

Despite his lasting reputation, Cornbury's spirit refuses to leave the city. He haunts it in his own peculiar fashion—taking notice of no one but stepping along as if he still ruled the city and has a royal sanction to

Opposite: The Cass Gilbert–designed U.S. Custom House pictured soon after its opening. Many find it puzzling that Cornbury has chosen to haunt a building that didn't exist when he was alive, but it must be remembered that the Custom House was built in a location of vital importance in seventeenth- and eighteenth-century New York. The Custom House is on the site of the original Fort Amsterdam, the walled seat of government of the old Dutch city before it was conquered by the British in 1664. By Lord Cornbury's time, the fort had been renamed Fort Anne and it was said that the governor was particularly fond of walking along its ramparts.

Edward Hyde Lord Cornbury,
afterw: 3rd Earl of Clarendon.

do with it whatever he wishes. In many ways his actions are as incomprehensible in death as they were in life.

Many thought that Cornbury was actually mad. In earlier years he had started a fistfight with his then-sovereign, James II, and he lived so lavishly beyond his means that he was eventually forced to flee to the New World to escape his creditors. He also had an odd fetish about women's ears. There

is a story that at a banquet welcoming him to the city, the new governor delivered an after-dinner speech extolling the beauty of his wife Katharine's ears and then invited the distinguished guests to file past and inspect them at close range.

This was a first taste of their governor's eccentricity, but matters were to become much worse. One night, an officer of the law apprehended what he took to be a

prostitute plying her trade on Broadway, only to find that the "lady" was in fact the governor of New York out for his daily stroll. Following the incident, Cornbury showed no shame whatsoever in appearing in his feminine finery whenever the whim took him, even during the somber opening of the New York Assembly. His peculiarity was noted by many contemporaries; Horace Walpole, for example, wrote of a conversation he had had with a New York friend by the name of George Williams. Williams recalled his father's experience of Lord Cornbury, saying that his father "has done business with Cornbury in women's clothes. He used to sit at the open window so dressed, to the great amusement of the neighbors. He employed always the most fashionable milliner, shoe maker, stay maker, etc."

Cornbury's response to the disgust that greeted his mode of dress was always the same and always delivered with the same sneer. His warped logic held that as he was the representative of Queen Anne, then he should represent her as faithfully as possible, in dress as in everything else. Such self-delusional justifications fooled no one.

There are a number of historical documents, letters, and diaries that refer to the old governor's fondness for gowns and bonnets, but perhaps the most conclusive piece of evidence is the portrait of Cornbury that is now one of the most popular pictures in the New York Historical Society's collection. The portrait, which does indeed bear a striking resemblance to Queen Anne, is said to have been sat for by Lord Cornbury. Beneath the figure appear the words "Edward Hyde Lord Cornbury, afterwards 3rd Earl of Clarendon." Some historians counter that Cornbury was the victim of a hate campaign, and that his depiction in female attire was a smear to discredit him personally, and through him British rule. However, this does not explain why those who have seen his ghost are able to identify the figure in the painting as the rather ugly woman they have seen on the steps of the Custom House, where 250 years after his death Cornbury can most often be found. Witnesses describe an odd-looking woman clad in the best fashion of the eighteenth century.

His wife was not much less disliked. Lady Cornbury had a way, when paying social calls on prominent citizens, of so praising certain of their choice possessions that they felt obliged to offer those items to her out of courtesy—and, of course, she never refused such generous gifts. It was said that shortly after the Cornburys arrived in New York City, wealthy locals took to hiding their best silver, china, and other valuables if they knew she was visiting.

But far more serious than tales of Lady Cornbury's greed and her husband's strange predilection for cross-dressing were the accusations against Cornbury for bad judgment in his political appointments and financial mismanagement of the colony's resources. With money put aside for strengthening the city's fortifications, he built a country home on a little islet in New York Harbor, then called Nutten Island, thereby giving it the name by which it is known today: Governor's Island. He was also accused of taking bribes and giving lucrative political jobs to those office-seekers most willing to make financial contributions to his lavish lifestyle as well as persecuting those who opposed him, particularly the Quakers.

Cornbury's reign of corruption was, however, relatively short-lived. After only four years in office, the New York and New Jersey assemblies over which he presided drew up a list of their grievances and petitioned the Board of Trade back in England to remove the pestilential figure. The situation came to the attention of the queen herself, who was adamant that Cornbury's relation to her should be no protection for a man who so violated her subjects. The assemblies were victorious, and Cornbury was evicted from his post and immediately thrown into a debtors' prison. Fortunately for him, his father died soon after, leaving the now ex-governor enough money to settle his debts and make his ignominious way back to the country of his birth, seething with rage at the treatment he had received in New York. He had also inherited this title upon his father's death and took his seat in the House of Lords. Showing more trust in him than did the colonists, Queen Anne later appointed him to other important positions. When he died in 1723, Cornbury was buried in his family's vault in Westminster Abbey.

If the manifestation seen in and around the former Custom House is indeed the wraith of its former governor and not the shade of some unattractive but forgotten woman who resembles Cornbury, then this is a haunting of particular interest. There are few reports of spirits traveling great distances from their remains, but Cornbury's bones are interred at Westminster Abbey in London. Why would a man so roundly despised in New York return again and again to the city?

One possibility is that he has come to seek his wife, whose shade is said to walk the churchyard of Trinity Church. Lady Cornbury died in New York before her husband was dismissed from office, and there is evidence that in spite of their unpleasant characters, they were a devoted couple. Perhaps, like the ghosts of many other lovers, he is drawn to his wife's last resting place.

Or perhaps Lord Cornbury is so scornful of New York and its people that he has crossed the Atlantic to once again arrogantly flaunt himself before them. Maybe he wishes to vex the colonists as much now as he did in the days when he would leap out on them in the street, screaming and laughing in his ribbons and bows. If so, and despite his many faults and sins, perhaps there is something to admire in a man so contemptuous of public opinion that he not only flaunted his transvestism during life, but now returns from the grave to do so again and again.

Or maybe the academics who have reappraised Cornbury's history are correct. Perhaps his sullied reputation is the result of a campaign to blacken his name and have him removed from office. Could it be that Cornbury was really a noble man, who returns from the grave dressed as a woman to draw attention to the injustice done to him? Maybe if this view becomes generally accepted, he will leave the Custom House. If that day comes, New York will lose one of its more colorful—and elegant—ghosts.

the wraiths of water street

bridge café—279 water street

Water Street, with its notorious waterfront taverns, dance halls, and brothels, was once one of the most fetid stews of human existence ever to have blighted the earth. A place of squalor and misery that was home to a few individuals who in life were more frightening than any character from a novel. That such people as Gallus Mag and Sadie the Goat existed at all is almost unbelievable, but their lives have been well documented and, of course, the skeptical can always take a midnight visit to this now innocuous-looking street. The spirits of its most brutal inhabitants are still with us, haunting the pavements and buildings where violence was once so casual. It is almost as though they were so vicious in life that even death wants nothing to do with them. With them walks at least one who met her end at the hands of one of New York's most grisly murderers.

Since its infancy New York has been a metropolis with a seamy side. For all its uptown glittering towers and fancy sophistication, it still has a bubbling history of violence and death just beneath the surface. Fiends and murderers have lived here as untouched by the law as they were by conscience. And of all the once-violent streets that are now a part of the famous South Street Seaport Historic District, none was more notorious than Water Street. Back in the eighteenth and early nineteenth centuries, life was more than just a little unsavory here, and it is, perhaps, no wonder that the sadistic denizens of the past have left an indelible mark on their neighborhood. Theirs were lives of drunkenness, disrepute, and spontaneous bloodshed. It was a

dangerous place, infused with the energy of New York's thriving seafaring industry and an ever-constant supply of recently arrived sailors prowling the streets in search of a drink, a fight, and a woman.

Even by the standards of Water Street, though, the two females we are about to meet were more than usually fierce when they were alive. And over the last two centuries there have been numerous eyewitnesses who attest that in the dead of night they have seen two hags matching their descriptions. And not only do their spirits walk, but—if we are to believe hearsay and urban myth—late-

Above: The Bridge Café, once the notorious Hole in the Wall, is sited at the corner of Water and Dover streets, just across from the moorings of the Brooklyn Bridge. Built in 1794, it is very likely the city's oldest continuously operating tavern and the old haunt of Gallus Mag.

Left: The busy street scene of merchants and traders plying their trade around the Tontine Coffee House, Water and Wall Streets, around 1797. This area was the home of many of New York's first gangs such as the Dead Rabbits, Bowery Boys, Gophers, Plug Uglies, and Five Pointers.

night passersby have had their arms jerked or felt some other unexplained violence in the vicinity. It seems that the passing of their physical bodies has not lessened the two women's glee in inflicting pain. Their spirits do not silently bemoan their fate or playfully move the furniture around; they delight in fear and violence now as they did in the days when America was a young republic and New York an expanding city of immigrants.

The first of our female devils is the ghostly form of the woman monster known as Gallus Mag, hailed in her dubious circles as the "Queen of the Waterfront." Gallus Mag was one of the fiercest women ever to tread the streets of the seaport, a notorious female bouncer who was employed by a waterfront dive called the Hole in the Wall— now the Bridge Café. One-armed Charley Monell, the proprietor of the Hole in the Wall, hired Mag to keep order in the tavern. Nicknamed "Gallus Mag" because of the

garters she wore (also called galluses), Mag was a burly English woman, standing six feet tall, who filed her teeth to points and had brass fingernails. She patrolled her territory with a knife in her pocket and a large bludgeon in one hand. If a customer at the Hole got too rowdy, he soon felt Mag's vengeance. She was particularly well known for ear biting and kept a trophy collection of severed ears preserved in alcohol in a jar above the bar. Recalls author Herbert Asbury:

It was her custom, after she'd felled an obstreperous customer with her club, to clutch his ear between her teeth and so drag him to the door, amid the frenzied cheers of the onlookers. If her victim protested, she bit his ear off, and having cast the fellow into the street she carefully deposited the detached member in a jar of alcohol behind the bar . . . She was one of the most feared

Left: The Bridge Café is at 279 Water Street on the corner of this group of buildings. Of equal historic importance is 273 Water Street, next to the Smith Freight Terminal. This is the third-oldest house in Manhattan and was built for sea captain Joseph Rose. In the 1860s it was home to Christopher (Kit) Burns's Sportsmen's Hall. Kit had been a leader of the infamous Dead Rabbits, the Five Points gang portrayed in the movie *The Gangs of New York*. The "sport" on exhibit at Kit's place was dog baiting: pitting terriers against large, vicious, hungry rats.

denizens on the waterfront, and the police of the period shudderingly described her as the most savage females they'd ever encountered.

Mag's wrath was not only directed at the drunken sailors who got out of hand in the bar. She had a well-publicized feud with the second of the two ghosts most often seen on Water Street—Sadie the Goat, leader of the terrifying river pirate gang the Daybreak Boys. After one extremely vicious fight, in which Sadie was deprived of one of her ears (it joined Mag's collection in the jar above the bar), Sadie fled the East River neighborhood and took up with a gang in the West Village. Later the two women made peace. When Sadie acknowledged Mag as the Queen of the Waterfront, Mag returned the severed ear, which Sadie enshrined in a locket she wore for the rest of her life.

Sadie saw the feud with Gallus Mag as just a minor setback in her criminal career. When on dry land, her ploy was to head butt innocent passersby and then call upon her gang to rob the victim as they reeled from the attack. And in the world of piracy, she was proud to be the leader of a gang who ruled with such fear. As Herbert Asbury explains:

> With the Jolly Roger flying from the masthead and Sadie the Goat pacing the deck in proud command, they sailed up and down the Hudson from the Harlem River to Poughkeepsie and beyond, robbing farmhouses and riverside mansions, terrorizing the hamlets, and occasionally holding men, women and children for ransom. It has been said that Sadie the Goat, whose ferocity far exceeded that of her ruffianly followers, compelled several men to walk the plank.

Most of New York's ghosts seem to have a reason to linger in the city; either an injustice or tragedy has befallen them, or their passion for the city has transcended even death. However, it appears that the only motive of these two despicable women is to continue their reign of terror. Perhaps in this they are not unlike ghostly actors, so famous in life that they prefer to stay on stage rather than accept their own demise. Maybe these women would rather remain as shades where their notoriety was once so great than to pass into the afterlife. If we make this assumption, it becomes less improbable that two such unlikely characters would choose to linger here. As has been discussed in one or two other stories in this book, it is also likely that for a spirit to make its presence felt, it would take great strength of will. We can safely assume that two women who could become so legendary for their cruelty in a world brimming with brutal men must have possessed incredible force of personality.

Gallus Mag and Sadie the Goat are not alone on Water Street. There have been many sightings here, unsurprising for a street with such a past. Few of the ghosts are regular and remain nameless; they are the spirits of long-forgotten people who perhaps died suddenly in some violent brawl or were the victims of the many murders the area witnessed. One such killing, however, was so grisly that the name of the victim and her appearance were headline news, which makes identifying her wraith easy. In the 1890s, even the life-hardened residents of this rough neighborhood were sent into a panic when the body of a middle-aged prostitute, Carrie Brown, was found in her room at a third-rate hotel at Front Street and Catherine Slip. Carrie, called "Old Shakespeare" because of her fondness for reciting the Bard when she was drunk, had not only been murdered; her body had been badly mutilated.

The grisly crime scene had many of the same features—the victim a streetwalker, the corpse cut up—as the Jack the Ripper murders that had so recently terrorized the citizens of London. The New York tabloids wasted no time in proclaiming that Jack had migrated to New York and was stalking the riverfront in search of fresh prey. Other strange murders occurred soon afterward (bodies found floating in the East River, for example), but the connection with the Ripper was only a theory. As in London, though, the murderer was never brought to justice. At least one of his victims still stalks the neighborhood. In recent times, there have been sightings of a mutilated woman stumbling along the darker side streets. Carrie Brown, like many other traumatized spirits, cannot or will not desert the place where she was so horribly put to death.

The unruly old days of the riverfront have gradually faded away, but there is a rich and wild history here, just below the surface. Though it may now be civilized, the waterfront is still home to the ghosts of the city's violent past. The wraith of Gallus Mag still strides along the dark streets and cuts a terrifying figure. She is still the Queen of the Waterfront, and woe betide anyone who dares challenge her.

Above: Water Street was not a place for the fainthearted in 1857, under the grip of gang warfare. Here the local Dead Rabbit gang is attacked on their barricade by the rival Bowery Boys.

speak softly (AND CARRY A BIG stick)!

THE POLICE BUILDING—240 CENTRE STREET

New York's finest are not renowned as having the kind of imaginations that manufacture hoaxes or apparitions. Which makes it extremely odd that a number of the officers who used to work at the old New York City Police Headquarters at 240 Centre Street all report a ghost in the building. And not just any old ghost, but the wraith of one of the United States' best loved presidents—Theodore Roosevelt.

At first glance, this seems like one of the more implausible ghost stories that you might read. After all, why would a man of such greatness in life choose to walk the corridors of the New York City Police Headquarters? Particularly when the building is one that he had no connection with in life.

But before it is dismissed, we should remember that at an earlier stage in his career Roosevelt served as the New York police commissioner. It was a job he undertook with typical enthusiasm. Although he only served as commissioner for two years, Roosevelt made sweeping changes to the department. Every morning he cycled to work from his sister's house on Madison Avenue, where he and his second wife, Edith, were temporarily living, to his office at 300 Mulberry Street. After work, he would tread the city's streets at night alone, making sure patrolmen were walking their beats as they should instead of occupying the local taverns. When Teddy took office, the police department was full of corruption from its top administrative officers down to the lowly rookie cop. Graft and kickbacks were everywhere, with policemen on the take from shopkeepers and salon owners. Roosevelt started his reform movement by firing two of the force's most infamous members. He also started paying attention to the problems of the poor and, along with his journalist friends Jacob Riis and Lincoln Steffens, exposed the deplorable living conditions of the disadvantaged. The measure of his success is undoubted; he left the city and its police force in far better shape than when he took office.

With this in mind, maybe it is not so odd that Roosevelt would wish to see how the work he started was being carried out. And the policemen's stories have the ring of authenticity about them. One officer tells how he was sitting in his office one night typing up a report when he slowly became aware that he was not alone. Looking up, he saw that a gentleman had appeared—a short, stubby man with ruddy cheeks and, despite his lack of stature, an imposing bearing. The policeman stopped typing and studied the shady figure. He thought he recognized him, but could not place him. It was only when the little man had disappeared back into the gloom that he realized where he had seen a similar person: in history books. His story is one among the many reports that all say the same thing. Police officers have looked up from their work to see the old president silently watching over them.

Whether this ghost story is some organized prank or genuine sightings of one of America's greatest men will remain a mystery, for the police headquarters moved once again and Roosevelt has yet to appear in the new building. The old building on

Centre Street has now been developed into luxury apartments, and none of the inhabitants have reported any paranormal disturbances from any of New York's dead politicians. That Theodore Roosevelt watches over the police force he helped to make into one of the finest in the world may seem a stretch of credulity. But if you can't trust a policeman, who can you trust?

Above: President Theodore Roosevelt, who was said to haunt the Centre Street headquarters of the New York Police Department during the 1970s. Does Teddy still patrol the halls of the old police headquarters? Or has he followed the department to their new home, keeping watch over the police force he helped create?

the wraith of melrose hall

THE WRAITH OF MELROSE HALL

Melrose Hall was the kind of house that might have been designed straight

from the pages of a Gothic novel. Beyond its otherwise normal appearance lay

another house entirely, one of labyrinthine hidden corridors, secret rooms, and

dungeons where Revolutionary soldiers once met to discuss strategy and

torture information from captured spies. As you might expect in such a house,

it also harbored a restless spirit: a woman who once starved to death here.

Before the old building was razed, many of the hall's inhabitants and neighbors

related the same blood-freezing story about the emaciated figure that often

appeared in the window of a room that no one could find the door to, unless,

of course, they followed the mournful cries through a secret door to the very

top of the house.

Classic ghost stories are surprisingly few and far between. At most the ghost hunter is usually left with a spirit whose motivations can only be guessed at, assembling the evidence from fragments of a life half forgotten and never truly known, perhaps added to slowly by investigators and mediums. Even then it is almost impossible to draw an accurate conclusion, for the spirit world seems to work on very different principles from our own. But the story of the ghost at Melrose Hall is different. We have the tale from the dying lips of the man who set the train of events in action. It has left us with a rarity: a ghost story that reads as if it were written by a novelist. This tale, however, is true. Along with the eyewitnesses who were there on the momentous evening of which you are about to read, other very credible citizens have told

Opposite: The celebrated actress and writer Anna Cora Mowatt, who bought Melrose Hall in 1836 and confirmed the presence of the house's resident specter.

120

of seeing the same figure at an upper window of the hall, while the house's inhabitants often reported hearing her cries.

Melrose Hall, near what is now Bedford Avenue, was one of the grandest old homes of pre-Revolutionary New York, a hub of Tory social life and the scene of legendary and lavish parties. It was built in 1749 by an Englishman named Lane and was one of the earliest examples of English architecture in the area, an indicator that New York's fortunes were on the rise, for few had built a private home on this scale before. Everything about it was ostentatious, particularly in contrast to the modest and staid Dutch farmhouses in the surrounding neighborhood. But besides its grandeur, Melrose Hall was also an architectural curiosity—an agglomeration of immense rooms, secret passages, and innumerable hiding places.

A massive oak door, double bolted and divided horizontally into two sections, opened on a wainscoted hall, extending the entire depth of the house, while in the center was a fireplace large enough to roast an ox. To the left, a broad mahogany staircase led to the rooms above. On each side of the house were large wings, the right containing the ballroom and banqueting hall and the left the dining rooms and library.

Not all was as it seemed, however. The house held secrets known only to a very few. A clandestine staircase, opening into a closet on one side of the fireplace in the hall, offered the only access to a chamber near the roof containing small stained-glass windows. And what appeared as a handsome buffet in the dining room was in reality a hidden door, moved by the action of a spring concealed in the panels, which opened onto a dark passage leading to the servants' quarters. All the upstairs apartments were connected by secret passages behind the panels and tapestry. And deep alcoves on the top floor afforded ample means of concealment to those who wished to come and go unobserved.

These private chambers and secret passages were reputedly installed by Colonel William A. Axtell, commander of colonial forces, who used the house not only for entertaining but for holding covert meetings with fellow Tories during the period of Revolutionary wartime hostilities. Of course the house's secrets must also have presented the opportunity for unseen dalliances and liaisons during parties and the occasional seduction of a kitchen maid.

As if these hidden rooms and doors were not sinister enough, Melrose Hall concealed even more baleful spaces. Beneath the mansion were dungeons and vaults, where prisoners were reputedly confined during the Revolution, and where the light of day never penetrated. After the death of Colonel Axtell, human bones were found in one of these dark cells. His clothing had long since moldered into dust, but his skeleton was entire, though the skull was fractured, whether from torture or in an attempt at suicide was not clear.

This then was Melrose Hall, a schizophrenic building that appeared all gaiety and light to the revelers who crowded its ballroom so often, but which was a veritable maze of secrets and deceptions. The house, in fact, was much like its owner, for Axtell too was a man who concealed his sins well by keeping them just out of sight behind the walls.

Surprisingly, considering the dark deeds that are said to have gone on in the hall's hidden spaces, only one of these rooms seems to have produced a ghost. It was in a concealed, attic chamber above the ballroom that Melrose Hall concealed its owner's greatest secret. For this single room was the abode of a woman whose existence was kept from the other members of the household. The mysterious lady made her appearance shortly before Colonel Axtell's arrival at Melrose Hall. The few who saw her later described the stranger as a tall, dark woman of wondrous beauty and kindly manner. But she disappeared as suddenly as she had arrived, and few remembered her until one fateful night in the future. She was, it transpired, Isabella, the colonel's live-in mistress. Once inside the house, she was smuggled through the secret passage into a room that she was never to leave alive again. That she seems to have been a willing participant in her own incarceration points to an incredible devotion to Axtell.

When the colonel moved into the mansion with his wife and two small children, they brought with them a retinue of domestic staff, among whom was an old and faithful servant named Miranda who had gained the confidence of her master. Apart from the colonel himself, this trusted retainer was the only person to know of the existence of the woman occupying the secret chamber. Immediately upon her arrival, the servant took charge of the welfare of the lodger and was the only member of the staff to visit her, bringing her meals prepared by her own hand to escape the notice of the other servants and carefully slipping up the stairs to the hidden chamber. Isabella's presence in the house was, of course, kept secret from the colonel's wife, allowing him to continue his illicit affair within the comfort of his family home. We can only imagine what Isabella's life must have been like, staring at the same walls or out of the tiny windows day after day while languidly waiting for her lover to slip away from his business and family below.

And so it went with Axtell leading a double life under one roof with some aplomb. Surely his wife must have thought him the most devoted of husbands who never left the house, but worked long into the night while she and the children slept. After a fashion, all was well at Melrose Hall.

Unfortunately, it was not to continue so. The story goes that when the colonel was unexpectedly called away to take command of a military campaign against the Native Americans, he realized that there was a greater danger of his affair being exposed. Knowing that he would be away for some time, he also became plagued with fear for Isabella. A premonition gripped him, and he became certain that if she stayed within the house, it would be her undoing. So, fearing for her life and his own exposure, he crept up to the chamber to ask her to abandon the secret hideout while he was away, and offered her money so that she could set herself up elsewhere in the neighborhood. Isabella indignantly spurned his offer, suspecting that he was trying to buy her silence and abandon her, so the colonel had no option but to allow her to remain in self-imposed imprisonment. To safeguard himself, however, he demanded that her door remain firmly locked and that she never attempt to leave the chamber. The old servant was entrusted with the key and given strict instruction never to allow her charge to roam free.

Colonel Axtell's tour of duty lasted a year, throughout which Isabella kept her vigil, waiting anxiously for the return of her lover and the regular unbolting of the door to her attic room by the old servant who brought her meals and kept her company. But only a week before the scheduled return of the master of the house, his old servant sickened and died. It is assumed that she made some last efforts to explain the nature of the hidden chamber, but her weakly spoken pleas would have been taken as the delirious wanderings of a senile mind. Isabella, unaware of her servant's death, patiently waited for her attendant's steps, but none came. And as the days passed, she began to realize her fearful fate, that the room where so many happy hours had been passed with her lover was soon to become her grave. So well hidden was it that her weakening screams of agonized panic were heard by no one. Without either food or water, she starved to death quickly.

On the night of the colonel's return, Melrose Hall was brilliantly lit, and a celebratory feast laid. It was not until close to midnight, however, that his carriage drew to a halt outside the imposing front door. Greeted by family and friends, he reveled in their admiration before seeking the first chance to make his way through the library into the servants' quarters to inquire of his faithful retainer. Only then did he learn the truth—that she had died the week before.

Knowing that he could not immediately excuse himself from the welcoming party to check on the well-being of his lover, the colonel stumbled back to his guests, sick with fear. As he entered the hall, he was frozen to the spot in terror. The gaiety and dancing had ceased, the candles had burned out, and in their place was a dim glow shining out

Opposite page: This rare photograph of the interior of Melrose Hall shows the stairs in the servants' quarters. From here the servant Miranda would steal to a secret room, bearing food for her master's illicit lover.

from the opened door to the secret passage. And accompanied by a low, unearthly sound, the spectral form of Isabella entered.

Her body was wasted, her face ashen pale, her long black hair hanging lifelessly over her cadaverous shoulders. The apparition bore the look of unutterable sorrow, and the hands were clenched in an attitude of woe. She wore a floating dress of ethereal white, and beneath her translucent skin every artery in her face could be seen. Noiselessly, she glided through the hall, one arm pointing toward the colonel's wife, while her glassy eyes remained fixed on her lover. One witness's story has her forming the word "betrayer" with an accusing finger before the spectral light faded and Isabella took her leave. For a few moments all was peaceful in the dark banqueting room, but then began an unearthly wail that echoed through the whole building. As it faded, an enormous thud was heard as if a body falling to the floor had been amplified many times over.

When candles were lit again, Colonel Axtell was found lying on the floor close to the entrance to the secret passage, a wound to his chest oozing blood. The maddened man had stabbed himself through the heart with his own sword. Not yet dead, he lingered for a few hours, during which time he managed to tell the story of Isabella's confinement. He also asked that his family move to England to escape the ignominy that his actions had brought upon their heads.

The shame that fell on the Axtell family meant that the full story of that night was hushed up. But gossip by guests and, in particular, by the servants meant that the chilling story of Isabella's revenge was told and retold in the ensuing years. Although, as is always the case when dealing with the supernatural, no hard evidence exists to confirm the identity of Isabella or the oft-recited details of her demise, the haunting of Melrose Hall is well documented. Strangely, it seems to have affected the residents of the surrounding neighborhood far more than the subsequent inhabitants of the house itself.

One owner, a Reverend Dr. Robinson, who owned Melrose Hall from 1845 to 1879, claimed that though he was aware of its existence, the ghost never bothered him because he was a sound sleeper who was in the habit of retiring for the night at an early hour. Reverend Robinson must have been a man of cool nerve indeed to sleep soundly under the same roof as this pitiful wretch. Another owner of the house, Anna Cora Mowatt, a well-known actress and writer, acknowledged the persistent local reports of the ghostly lady. The Mowatts, who purchased the property in 1836 and owned it for five years, gave the house its popularly accepted name of Melrose Hall because of the numerous rose bushes covering the grounds. In her autobiography, Anna Mowatt gave the following description:

There were dark and spacious vaults beneath the kitchen, where it was said that prisoners had been confined, and there was a secret chamber above the great ballroom, to which no access could be found, save by a small window. The neighbors affirmed that a young girl had been purposely starved to death in that chamber, and that her ghost wandered at night about the house. Indeed, this report had gained such credence that nothing could have induced many of the older inhabitants of the village to pass a night beneath the haunted roof.

They had reason to fear the place, for there were many among them who had seen her pale form against the same small upstairs window since the night when Isabella appeared before the assembled company at the hall. The sighting always provoked terror and dread, precisely what Axtell's mistress must have felt as the gnawing pain of hunger and thirst gradually took her life. For well over a century, residents of Flatbush, in the present-day borough of Brooklyn, avoided the area surrounding the building after dark, fearful of the cries that could be plainly heard from the road in front of the mansion.

Colonel Axtell himself seems to have gone quietly to the grave. As the instigator of this terrible tragedy, he might be expected to have shared in Isabella's curse, to constantly walk the site of her death. But either the conscience that allowed him to secrete a mistress just steps away from where his children played is uncaring enough to leave Isabella to her fate, or his shame is such that he cannot bear to show his face.

Following the Mowatts, Melrose Hall went through a succession of owners until 1883, when it came into the possession of Dr. Homer Bartlett, who demolished the wings and relocated the main section of the house four hundred feet back from its original location. The remaining structure was torn down in 1905 for the expansion of Bedford and Parkside Avenues. Reports of the ghost of Melrose Hall vanished along with the house. Perhaps with the destruction of the house, Isabella's soul felt free to move on.

Such events seem too close to fiction to have any basis in reality, yet there is at least some truth here. Various subsequent owners uncovered the secrets Melrose Hall had hidden behind its walls, and Axtell's wife and children did indeed move to England shortly after his funeral. Even then there was gossip of some strange occurrence at the hall. The ghostly story has been passed down from mouth to mouth over the decades, presumably gathering embellishment with each telling, but perhaps at its core is some truth. Nevertheless, the hall is now gone and all that is left are rumors and the tales of scared neighbors who told of seeing Isabella's ghostly form framed against the window of the room where she died.

mURDeReD By a gHOSt

There are few more chilling prospects than revenge from beyond the grave.
The idea of a corpse reanimated—no longer constrained by physical laws and
filled with hatred, stalking its victim wherever she goes—is one on which many
horror movies are based. Fortunately, such tales are few in reality, and almost
all of these are easily disprovable. This story then is an exception. What you
are about to read is not only documented, but is referred to in police records
as unsolvable and unexplainable. It is a very real "X-File," and its protagonists
were as strange in life as they proved to be in death.

The beginning of the story lies in the late 1860s, and to the casual observer there would seem to be nothing about the charming pair strolling the decks of the stately liner—an elegant lady and her diminutive ward—that would spawn such horror in later years. The woman and child were well known to the crews of the ocean liners on which they regularly sailed. Introducing herself as Mrs. Ada Danforth, the older woman explained to them that her little blonde companion, Fanchon Moncare, was an orphan whose parents had died. On her eighteenth birthday, she would inherit a fortune, but meanwhile Ada was her legal guardian. Thus they excited little notice among the people with whom they traveled.

The little girl was a cherub who went nowhere without her precious china doll. On board the ship she would curtsey adorably to any inquiring passenger and skip away, and when the ship docked in New York she would play happily around Mrs. Danforth in the customs hall, still clutching her precious doll. None of the customs officers ever thought to stop the beautiful little girl and check her plaything. Perhaps if they had, they might have prevented one of New York's most grisly hauntings, and also caught two of the city's most clever criminals.

Opposite: The interior of New York's notorious Tomb Prison at around the time that Estelle Ridley would have been incarcerated here. Ridley took her own life in the jail and soon afterward returned from the grave to take vengeance on her mortal enemy, Magda Hamilton.

Above: The original Tombs Prison, with the replacement building in the background, circa 1905. To the left is New York's own "Bridge of Sighs," through which the prisoners were led to their cells.

For their identities were pure fiction. Fanchon's real name was Estelle Ridley—and she was a 43-year-old circus midget. And Ada Danforth was not her guardian but her partner in crime. Arriving in New York at the end of their annual trip from Paris via the French port of Cherbourg, they would travel on to Staten Island to open the pleasant waterfront home they used every summer. Sometime shortly afterward, they would take a ferry back to Manhattan and a cab into New York's Chinatown, where an elderly Chinese friend, Wing To, waited to receive them. In his back room, the head of "Fanchon's" favorite doll would be unscrewed and a fortune in gems spilled out, the harvest of several months' larceny in Europe. On one trip alone, the haul in precious stones was worth $250,000.

This profitable business might have gone on for years with no consequences other than a few wealthy Europeans being relieved of their jewels, but for two factors: greed and romance.

Danforth and Ridley had been operating their transatlantic business under the protection of the "Tweed Ring," a corrupt band of city officials who took orders from William Marcy Tweed, boss of Tammany Hall. The organization had fingers in every scam in the city and are believed to have stolen as much as $200 million from the New York treasury between 1865 and 1871. Danforth and Ridley paid their dues to the Tweed Ring to allow them to continue their activities without any danger of apprehension. Danforth used this criminal license to establish herself in New York society from her base on her Staten Island estate. Ridley, however, had more down-to-earth tastes, and, as soon as she was able, dropped the act of sweet, rosy-cheeked little girl to become the hard-drinking, foul-mouthed adult who would find company in the Bowery saloons and at the Rockaway Park racetrack. It was there that she met another associate of the Tweed Ring, an attractive libertine named Magda Hamilton. The pair got on famously and planned to set up in business together as confidence tricksters and jewel thieves.

The evil duo's first target was a Chicago millionaire. Ridley and Hamilton duped him into allowing them into his home and parted him from $350,000 before fleeing back to New York. But the women soon fell out— first over the split of their ill-gotten fortune, and then over a love rival.

Estelle Ridley had fallen for the charms of a high-stakes gambler named Dartney Crawley, and she entered into a deadly feud for his affections with the rather more attractive Magda Hamilton. It is not known quite what happened between the two as they fought over the gambler's affection, but the episode ended with Hamilton vowing to seek revenge. And before the year was out, she was able to take it.

After the Chicago job, Ridley rejoined Danforth for yet another two-way Atlantic crossing. In the south of France in the spring of 1871, they ingratiated themselves with a French nobleman and hired two thugs to burgle his home in Marseilles. In the course of the robbery, their victim was assaulted and later died. Danforth and Ridley swiftly booked passage back to New York.

But when their steamship, the *Atlantic Star*, docked at the pier adjacent to Desbrosses Street, the police were waiting for them. Magda Hamilton had tipped them off, and, for the first time ever, Estelle Ridley's doll was inspected and the pair were incarcerated in the notorious Tombs Prison to await trial. Estelle provided the most dramatic moment of the ensuing court case. When she saw the gloating Magda sitting in the packed courtroom, Estelle sprang to her feet and made a shrill vow that she would one day kill her betrayer. Since Estelle had an impressive criminal record, she was sentenced to life imprisonment. Ada Danforth, ten years younger, was jailed as an accessory for twenty years.

Triumphantly, Magda married Dartney Crawley. He deserted her six months later to try his luck in a California mining venture, but the divorce settlement was generous and Magda was left very comfortably off. Her prosperity grew through shrewd investments, and she became a prominent figure in New York café society. When Mrs. Danforth's Staten Island home was put up for sale, the buyer was none other than Magda Hamilton, using the name Mrs. Dartney Crawley to hide her identity.

Estelle Ridley was soon all but forgotten by everyone until one morning Hamilton burst into police headquarters and cursed the officers for not letting her know that the prisoner had escaped. She explained that she had awakened from a heavy sleep to find her love rival in her bedroom. She said Estelle still wore her childish finery and clutched a big china doll, but she was now a bent and withered hag, grinning with toothless gums.

Magda had fled screaming into the bathroom, where she had locked the door and cowered for the rest of the night. Finally she found the courage to leave the room, and, at daybreak, she arrived at the police station in a state of hysteria and insisted on adequate protection until the little monster was recaptured and taken back to prison. It seems that that night Estelle was only playing with her victim, wanting her to find out the full horror of her appearance.

At the police station, a bemused sergeant produced a week-old copy of the *New York Sun*. He pointed to a short item on the back page reporting that Estelle Ridley, otherwise known as Fanchon Moncare, had hanged herself in her cell.

Hamilton was utterly terrified, insisting that she had seen her former partner with her own eyes, and that she must be alive and that the suicide was part of some elaborate escape plan. However, all inquiries supported the newspaper story. Estelle Ridley was certified as dead.

We can only imagine the dread experienced by Magda Hamilton. At least in her fright the previous night she must have had the comforting thought that if she could get away from the house, the police would protect her or that she could find some cunning place to hide. To realize that Ridley was seeking her blood even in death must have driven her almost to insanity with fear. On leaving the police station she immediately made every effort she could to run from her tiny nemesis, booking passage for Europe on a Cunard liner. Since the ship was to leave the next day, she had a farewell dinner with a friend and then went home, perhaps having convinced herself over dinner with some relaxing wine that her sleeping imagination must have been playing tricks.

On the next day, the servants found her trunks neatly packed, but there would be no ocean voyage for Magda. The woman was sprawled half-naked on the bed, her eyes protruding, and with congealed blood at the corners of her mouth. According to the medical examiner, she had drowned in her own blood. The membrane of her throat was ruptured as if some heavy object had been rammed into it with savage force.

The murder weapon was never found, but there was a clue of sorts. Lodged in Magda's bloody mouth were several hairs, similar to those found on the head of a child's china doll.

During the night, she had been visited again by the dead and wizened Estelle, and this time the ghost had taken full vengeance on her betrayer. Perhaps she woke from her sleep again to find the tiny apparition looming over her. Perhaps she struggled once again to the sanctuary of the bathroom. If so, it was to no avail: Estelle left her old partner as dead as she had promised that day in court. As dead as she was herself.

It might be hypothesized that this was all part of an elaborate plan hatched by Ridley before her death; she was an experienced and resourceful criminal with many contacts in the underworld, after all. It is not beyond the realms of plausibility that she came in contact with another female midget in the penal system, perhaps older and toothless. She might even have secured her services as an assassin, possibly directing the woman to a secret stash of money or jewels that Ridley

had made earlier in her career in payment for her services. Having all those years with nothing to do but plot revenge, it is surely feasible that she timed her own suicide to coincide with the appearance of this other woman in Hamilton's bedroom attired to look like herself and using a weapon that Magda Hamilton would surely recognize.

However, if these events can be ascribed to some twisted—but human—plot, it does not explain the experiences of later owners of Magda Hamilton's house. The site of this crime, known in the late 1800s as "the Crawley House," was never subsequently occupied for long. Tenants were terrified by the sound of a woman cursing in the night, using exactly the kind of language one might expect from a denizen of New York's lower drinking establishments. And, on one occasion, an officer of the New York Port authority reported seeing a diminutive figure on the balcony of the now-derelict home. Perhaps the price that Estelle Ridley paid for her reappearance in the mortal world was having to remain here in spirit forever. If so, she must have thought that it was a price worth paying to serve a one-time friend with her just deserts. Long before the house was abandoned, though, the police closed the file on one of the most bizarre cases in criminal history, and it remains unsolved to this day. The only evidence is from the victim herself, and, if we believe Magda Hamilton, her killer was a ghost.

THE CURSE OF THE GHOST IN THE WELL

MANHATTAN BISTRO—129 SPRING STREET

In the basement of the fashionable Manhattan Bistro on Spring Street is a deep old well that can trace its history back over two hundred years. In its depths once floated the mortal remains of Guliana Elmore Sands. Although her poor young murdered body has long since been removed and all the controversy surrounding the trial of her murderer forgotten, Guliana's spirit still resides here and creeps from her dark watery grave to visit her destructive anger on staff and customers of the restaurant.

That there is a supernatural force inhabiting the Manhattan Bistro is incontestable. Why else would lights turn on and off by themselves, plates come crashing to the floor, and ashtrays launch themselves at the walls? That the presence is that of Guliana (also called Elma by some) is now so well established that she is the only ghost to be mentioned in a landmark designation report. Her voice can sometimes be heard, calling mournfully to someone, though the name of the person she seeks is never quite clear enough to distinguish. Over the years, occultists, paranormal experts, and other interested parties have all attested that this is

all the work of a murdered young woman and that the focus of her energy lies at the bottom of the deep well in the basement.

It is not difficult then to trace this particular ghost back to a sensational murder trial that took place at the turn of the nineteenth century.

It was as New Yorkers bustled through bitterly cold streets at the end of December 1799 that Guliana, a pretty twenty-one-year-old milliner, failed to arrive at the boarding house owned by her aunt and uncle. As the police conducted a search and began inquiries, there was talk she had been kidnapped by a fellow boarding house guest

Opposite: Celebrated New York lawyer Alexander Hamilton (standing on the right with arm outstretched) speaks during the trial of Levi Weeks for the murder of Guliana Sands. So incensed was the public that Weeks was acquitted that he was publically insulted outside the courthouse. One of Sands's friends is said to have put a curse on Hamilton, which bore awful fruit a few years later when he was killed in a duel by Aaron Burr, with whom he teamed up to defend Weeks.

or even snatched from streets so crowded that no one could have heard her cries. One thing was certain: Guliana was gone, and despite the exhaustive hunt by her family and friends and the efforts of the police, no trace could be found of her.

It was a fraught Christmas that year in the little boarding house, and one from which her aunt and uncle, with whom she had lived for some time, were never to recover. Their grief was completed when Guliana's battered body was discovered in the well on Spring Street shortly after the bells sounded in the New Year of 1800. In those days it had not been built over and stood in the corner of a meadow. From it her body was pulled, as cold as the winter. One bystander later described that her corpse "was horrid enough—her hat and cap off, her hair hanging all over her head, her comb was yet hanging in her hair, tied with a white ribbon; her shawl was off; her gown was torn open with great violence, and her shoes were off." Although lacking the forensic skills of today, the coroner was able to determine that Guliana did not simply fall in and drown. She had been strangled and then thrown down the well. The search for a lost young woman instantly became a murder investigation.

Original suspicions that Guliana had died at the hands of someone familiar with the boarding house were renewed. Fingers pointed at Levi Weeks, a young man who resided there and who had become especially friendly with Guliana. Friends of the two even suggested they had been secretly betrothed, a notion denied by Levi Weeks.

What no one could prove was whether Levi was in Guliana's company in her last hours. They had not been seen leaving the boarding house together on the night she disappeared. And Levi named his brother Ezra Weeks as an alibi. Levi said he had visited Ezra on the night in question, and because this was some distance away, he could not possibly have been responsible for Guliana's death. However, there were persistent rumors that suggested that Weeks was being less than totally honest. Despite his well-known friendship with Guliana, it was claimed that he had asked one of her cousins to sign an affidavit testifying that he "paid no more particular attention to Guliana than to any other female in the house."

Investigators into the crime found witnesses who recalled seeing sleigh tracks in the snow around the well on the night of Guliana's death. They quickly formed the belief that Levi had hired a horse-drawn sleigh, kidnapped Guliana, and killed her, dumping her body down the well and setting off for his brother's home to create his alibi. He had plenty of time to do all that, they said. And besides, they couldn't find anyone else on whom to pin the blame.

Ezra Weeks was determined to prove his younger brother's innocence. A prominent Manhattan builder, Ezra had enough money to secure the services of topflight lawyers to handle the case. The team he hired was made up of Alexander Hamilton, Aaron Burr, and Brockholst Livingston. Although Burr and Hamilton were fierce enemies, they managed to work well enough together to hash out a strategy that would secure Weeks's innocence. They said Guliana was promiscuous and that she committed suicide when Weeks withdrew his proposal. Such was their brilliant case for the defense that the jury took just thirty minutes to declare Levi Weeks not guilty.

It was not a verdict that satisfied the family and friends of poor Guliana Elmore Sands. How, they asked, could Guliana have strangled herself before throwing herself down a well? And why would anyone choose such a horrible suicide, treading water until they became too tired or cold to carry on, then drowning in the freezing water? As the three lawyers left the court, they were jostled and insulted. "How could you let a guilty man go?" the crowd shouted. "We will allow you no peace for the rest of your lives!" One of Guliana's friends, Catherine Ring, was so disturbed by the verdict—and Hamilton's role in securing it—that she screamed at him: "If thee dies a natural death, I shall think there is no justice in Heaven." If this was a curse, it served its purpose, as you can read in Hamilton's own story.

Levi Weeks was so hounded by the public and press that he was forced to flee to Natchez, Mississippi. His forced exit did him no long-lasting harm, however, as he went on to become a prominent businessman.

Meanwhile, the case gradually drifted from popular memory, and as New York grew, even the well itself was swallowed up in the basement of the building that is now the bistro. For almost two decades, the room was filled with dirt concealing the historic well. And it would have remained hidden had not the bistro owner, Marie DaGrossa, one day decided to make more living space for herself. When she found the well, she knew she had something of historic value and called in the Landmarks Conservancy. It was then that Ms. DaGrossa learned why her bistro was haunted.

Guliana had refused to rest in peace. Though no one had yet made the connection with the well, so lost in history had the case become, the bistro suffered frequent visits from its occupant. Along with the sound of her voice calling, possibly to Weeks himself, she moved among the tables of the bistro, tipping a plate here and throwing an ashtray there, and occasionally touching diners with fingers icy from her sojourn at the bottom of her dark grave. We shall probably never know whether Weeks was guilty of her murder or not, but Guliana remains, perhaps furious that she was killed just before her marriage was supposed to take place, perhaps just angry that no one was brought to justice for her brutal slaying.

the mysteries of clinton court

the mysteries of clinton court

420–422 west forty-sixth street

Why he is here, no one can remember, but the ghost known as "Old Moor"

haunts the top of a set of stairs down the side of an old stable building in

Clinton Court. While some say that the deaths on those stairs are

coincidental, others are convinced that the woman and child who plunged to

their deaths and joined Old Moor in eternity did so recoiling in horror from

the apparition that suddenly appeared before them. It is a conviction that is

supported by the work of paranormal investigators and psychics who maintain

that Clinton Court is an area of "intense paranormal activity."

Clinton Court is a secret place; most people walking along West Forty-sixth Street, headed toward the two blocks of eating places designated "Restaurant Row," would pass by the private courtyard without even noticing its locked gate. Behind it is a courtyard and two houses, an eighteenth-century carriage house and an 1840s house. It is here that the ghost of Old Moor is said to have murdered a Danish woman, wife to Governor George Clinton's coachman, in the

1820s. If the stories are to be believed, she was walking up the outside stairs to the living quarters above the stables when the specter appeared before her. The woman was so terrified that she tumbled off the stairs and plunged to her death in the courtyard below.

From that time on, those stairs have been the focal point of Clinton Court's ghostly activity.

At first, no one knew who this presence was or that he was responsible for the poor

Opposite: George Clinton, the last British governor of New York and also the first governor under the new United States. The living quarters above the carriage house were occupied in the 1820s by Clinton. Of all the ghosts that swarm through the court, his is a notable absence, as it would seem likely that he would be called back here by the presence of one of his grandchildren who fell to her death on the stairs inhabited by Old Moor.

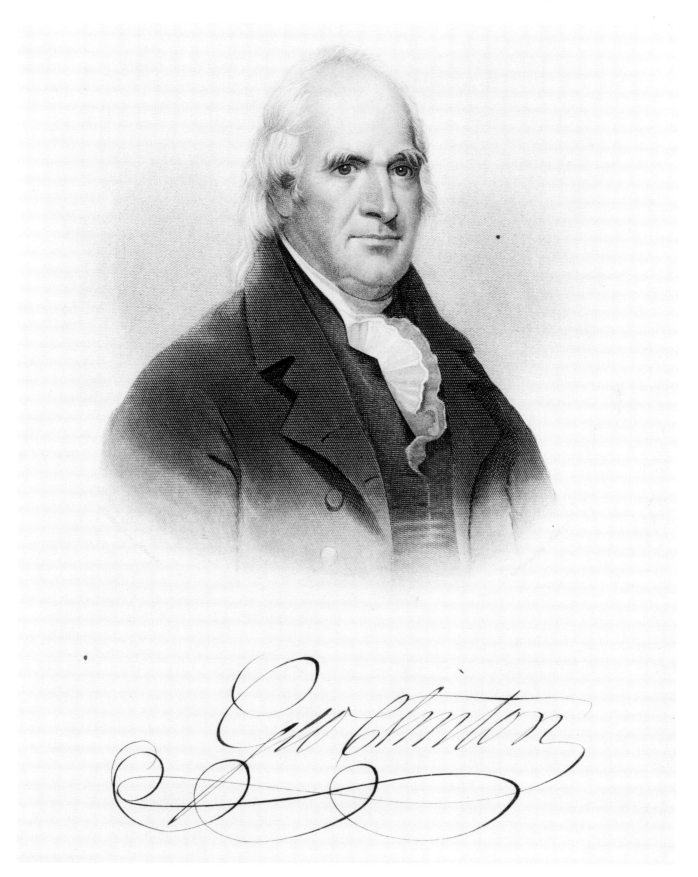

woman's death, but due to the efforts of mediums and psychics, including the famous Hans Holzer, he has been identified as Old Moor, a renegade sailor, so called because of his swarthy complexion. The sailor had been found guilty of mutiny and hanged at the battery, today's Battery Park at the southern tip of Manhattan. For some reason that even the psychics were unable to assess, his spirit had become attached in death to Clinton Court. Perhaps his reason for murder was loneliness, for the Dutchwoman whom he literally scared to death also remains, along with one other poor victim.

Of course, no one will ever know the truth of what happened among George Clinton's grandchildren as they played in the courtyard. We do know that they were playing a game called "ghost," throwing sheets over their heads and chasing one another around the courtyard. It could have been the sheet that tripped one of the little girls as she raced up the same steps. Or perhaps their childish game angered the genuine specters: even in those days the children knew enough of their history to name them the "scary stairs," and some said the girl, too, had encountered the scarred and gnarled face of Old Moor. Whatever happened, the child fell in exactly the same way as the coachman's wife and broke her neck on the ground below. After her death, the child joined the other two lost souls to reside at Clinton Court in spooky eternity.

As time went by, the downstairs stable at the carriage house was turned into living quarters, the entrance behind the arches closed, and the whole building turned into a private house. It was in the mid-nineteenth century, when the Hell's Kitchen area was first developed, that the second house was built. It faced the courtyard and, like the carriage house, was accessible through a narrow passage leading off West Forty-sixth Street. Over the years, both buildings have had many occupants who have experienced strange and sometimes chilling encounters with the paranormal.

Several people who have lived at the old carriage house have reported stepping outside on a wind-free day only to have the door slammed shut behind them. Another couple often heard strange tapping sounds on the roof that they described as sounding like a shower of small pebbles. When they went outside to investigate, they found no cause for the noise. And a lady who came to house-sit for two of the old stable's residents reported strange behavior from her two dogs. Every morning, although they were eager to go out for a walk, they would scamper to the top of the stairs and refuse to go any further. The animals cowered and shook with fright, and their owner had to scoop them up in her arms and carry them down the stairs.

The spirits, it seems, abound in Clinton Court. It was during the 1960s that the famous ghost-chaser Hans Holzer was called in to conduct one of his séances. During his time here, he contacted several spirits. Keeping company with the three ghosts on the stairs were a Revolutionary War soldier and another spirit that we met earlier in the book. "Hungry Lucy," it seems, had not vanished into the afterlife from June Havoc's house, but merely moved along.

Whether Holzer only contacted a few of the court's denizens or the spectral population is in a state of flux, the ghosts we have met here already are by no means the last. A latter-day resident of the converted carriage house, Tom Winberry, told how he was once awakened by a shadowy specter of a hooded woman hovering over his bed. Said Winberry: "I was intrigued but I didn't feel threatened. It finally dissipated after two or three minutes. To this day, I still don't know what it was. Take your pick: it was either an optical illusion, a hallucination, or a ghost." His wife has also told of strange visitations and describes spirits that do not seem to be Old Moor or any of the coterie already identified here. She attests that she has witnessed apparitions on at least two occasions, and there have been other unexplained happenings—such as a sudden plague of flying ants in the couple's living room. But Tom Winberry tried to be philosophical about his haunted home. "If there are spirits here, they've made peace and are probably gone," he said. "We've come to learn that when you live in a haunted house,

even the scurrying of mice can seem ominous."

Who is to say, of course, that it was mice the Winberrys heard in their home in Clinton Court, one of the most haunted sites in New York? Other inhabitants have given similar tales over the years; some of the spirits seem permanent, while others are merely passing through.

Why the court should be such a locus of paranormal activity is a mystery. Some imaginative spiritualists maintain that there are points in the physical world that are closer to the spiritual plane, allowing more spirits through. Of course this is impossible to prove or disprove, but it would follow that such places would be more heavily populated by ghosts than others. It is certainly odd that such a seemingly innocuous place as Clinton Court should be so rich in hauntings.

If we suspend disbelief for one moment and try to imagine that such a weak point in the fabric of reality does exist here, it must be teeming with the souls of the dead. For one thing is certain. If New York City is a typical example, then the world is full of ghosts, maybe too weak to make their presence felt anywhere but at such points though always with us, usually just beyond perception, desperate to take some part again in the great swirl of life.

INDEX

Picture Acknowledgments

R = Right L=Left C=Center T=Top B= Bottom

© **Algonquin Hotel, New York City** (www.thealgonquin.net): 79, 81.

© **Chrysalis Image Library:** 24, 37, 43, 47, 49, 65, 69, 87, 103, 104.

© **CORBIS:** 107, 130. / © Bettmann/CORBIS 1, 10, 32, 40, 55R, 57, 63, 71, 77, 78, 83, 85, 89, 95, 108, 109, 129. / © Hulton–Deutsch Collection/CORBIS 25. / © Lee Snider/Photo Images/CORBIS 33, 99. / © Underwood & Underwood/CORBIS 35, 93. / © Oscar White/CORBIS 50. / © G.E. Kidder Smith/CORBIS 53. / © John Springer Collection/CORBIS 75. / © Robert Holmes/CORBIS 92. / © Michael S. Yamashita/CORBIS 97. / © Thomas A. Kelly/CORBIS 113. / © Historical Picture Archive/CORBIS 121.

© **Jeff Towns/Dylans Bookstore Collection:** 2, 8, 59.

© **James Brown House:** 19, 20, 21.

Library of Congress, Prints and Photographs Division: [LC-US262-74620] 7. / [HABS, NY,31-NEYO,2-2] 15. / [HABS, NY,31-NEYO,2-43] 16. / [HABS, NY,31-NEYO,2-5] 17. / [LC-G612-T01-44213] 28. / [LC-USZ62-88103] 36T. / [LC-USZ62-42479] 36B. / [LC-USZ62-8322] 44. / [HABS,NY,31-NEYO,29-1] 55L. / [LC-USZ62-115942] 60. / [LC-D4-18607] 73. / [LC-USZ62-103985] 84. / [LC-USZ62-130157] 91. / [LC-G613-T- 58222] 101. / [LC-USZ62-74710] 105. / [LC-USZ62-98020] 114. / [HABS NO-NY-5686-1] 115. / [LC-USZ62-122057] 117. / 119 [LC-DIG-cwpbh-03437]. / [HABS, NY,31-NEYO,51-6] 124. / [LC-USZ62-117938] 135. / [LC-USZ62-110647] 139.

Library of Congress, Geography and Map Division: 13.

© **Museum of the City of New York:** 23, 27, 39, 66.

© **Merchant's House Museum:** 30.